MENU

Modernism
reimagined

Modernism reimagined draws inspiration
from the late modernists of our time to create
beautifully designed products and clever
solutions for modern living. The collection,
now featuring new furniture additions, is
made up of carefully considered pieces
that are both pure and minimalistic while
integrating richness and depth.

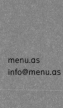
menu.as
info@menu.as

Godot 01, 3 Seater, Hallingdal 65, 130 (grey)
Godot 01, 1 Seater, Gaja C2C, 66061 (blue)
Iskos-Berlin

Peek Floor Lamp, White
Jonas Wagell

Tactile Vase Wide, Stainless Steel
Tactile Bowl, Stainless Steel
Gam Fratesi

Optical Candle Holder, White
Stokke Austad

Shrine, White
Note Design Studio

New Norm Bowl, Ø7.5 cm, White
Norm Architects

KVADRAT / RAF SIMONS

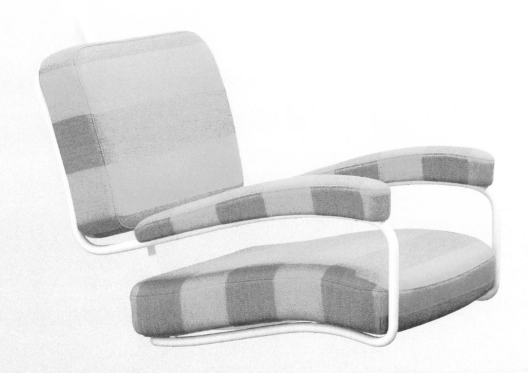

Polder Sofa Developed by Vitra in Switzerland, Design: Hella Jongerius

Go to www.vitra.com/dealer to find Vitra retail partners in your area.

vitra.

Reform

Reform collaborates with
internationally acclaimed
architects to redesign
your IKEA® kitchen

www.reformcph.com

Reform kitchen by Norm Architects

KINFOLK

Published by Ouur Media
Amagertorv 14, Level 1
1160 Copenhagen, Denmark
Telephone: +45 33 30 03 33

5210 N Williams Avenue
Portland, Oregon 97217 USA
Telephone: + 01 503-946-8400

Kinfolk is a slow lifestyle magazine published by
Ouur that explores ways for readers to simplify
their lives, cultivate community and spend more
time with their friends and family.
www.kinfolk.com

Ouur is a lifestyle publisher and agency
creating print and digital media for a young
creative audience.
www.ouurmedia.com

Printed in Canada

Publication Design by Charlotte Heal
Cover Photograph by Pelle Crépin

MADE & CRAFTED™
LEVI'S®

NATHAN WILLIAMS
Editor in Chief & Creative Director

GEORGIA FRANCES KING
Editor

ANJA VERDUGO
Art Director

CHARLOTTE HEAL
Design Director

DOUG BISCHOFF
Business Operations

NATHAN TICKNOR
Operations Manager

KATIE SEARLE-WILLIAMS
Business Manager

JESSICA GRAY
Communications Director

AMY WOODROFFE
Publishing Director

PAIGE BISCHOFF
Accounts Payable & Receivable

PAMELA MULLINGER
Advertising Director

RACHEL HOLZMAN
Copy Editor

RACHEL EVA LIM
Contributing Editor

JOHN CLIFFORD BURNS
Contributing Editor

JULIE CIRELLI
Contributing Editor

ANDREA SLONECKER
Recipe Editor

KELSEY BURROW
Proofreader

MARIO DEPICOLZUANE
Ouur Designer

CAROLYNE RAPP
Ouur Art Director

JESSE HIESTAND
Web Administrator

SHELBY HARTNESS
Operations Assistant

MOLLY MANDELL
Editorial Assistant

JAKOB HOVE
Design Assistant

KELLY ONGKOWIDJOJO
Art Assistant

LIELA TOURÉ
Marketing Assistant

———

SUBSCRIBE
KINFOLK IS PUBLISHED FOUR TIMES A YEAR
TO SUBSCRIBE, VISIT WWW.KINFOLK.COM/SUBSCRIBE OR EMAIL US AT SUBSCRIBE@KINFOLK.COM

CONTACT US
IF YOU HAVE QUESTIONS OR COMMENTS, WRITE TO US AT INFO@KINFOLK.COM
FOR ADVERTISING INQUIRIES, GET IN TOUCH AT ADVERTISING@KINFOLK.COM

www.kinfolk.com

www.lapaz.pt

ISSUE TWENTY CONTRIBUTORS

ALI & ANIKO
Stylists
Budapest, Hungary

TRAVIS ELBOROUGH
Writer
London, United Kingdom

NOEL MANALILI
Photographer
Paris, France

HELENA ARIZA
Photographer
New York, New York

KEITH FLANAGAN
Writer
Brooklyn, New York

ADRIENNE MATEI
Writer
Vancouver, Canada

MAKO AYABE
Translator
Tokyo, Japan

NICOLE FRANZEN
Photographer
Brooklyn, New York

CARA PARKS
Writer
New York, New York

KYLE BEAN
Set Designer
London, United Kingdom

ANNE FULLERTON
Writer
Sydney, Australia

ANDERS SCHØNNEMANN
Photographer
Copenhagen, Denmark

NEIL BEDFORD
Photographer
London, United Kingdom

ANJA GILDUM
Casting Director
Paris, France

MIE TAKAMATSU
Translator
Melbourne, Australia

SOFIE BRÜNNER
Set Designer
Copenhagen, Denmark

STEFAN HEINRICHS
Photographer
Berlin, Germany

AARON TILLEY
Photographer
London, United Kingdom

DIANA BUDDS
Writer
Brooklyn, New York

MARIANO HERRERA
Photographer
Barcelona, Spain

ZOLTAN TOMBOR
Photographer
Brooklyn, New York

SARAH BUNTER
Casting Director
London, United Kingdom

CARL HONORÉ
Writer
London, United Kingdom

FREDERIK VERCRUYSSE
Photographer
Antwerp, Belgium

ALICE CAVANAGH
Writer
Paris, France

KAORI ITO
Photographer
Tokyo, Japan

ALPHA VOMERO
Stylist
New York, New York

KATRIN COETZER
Illustrator
Cape Town, South Africa

KRISTOFER JOHNSSON
Photographer
Stockholm, Sweden

TAYLOR WEIK
Writer
Orange County, California

DUSTIN COSENTINO
Writer
Brooklyn, New York

MIKKEL KARSTAD
Food Stylist
Copenhagen, Denmark

RAHEL WEISS
Photographer
London, United Kingdom

PELLE CRÉPIN
Photographer
London, United Kingdom

ÅKE E:SON LINDMAN
Photographer
Stockholm, Sweden

DIANA YEN
Recipe Writer
Brooklyn, New York

arjowiggins

International standards
for creative papers

Standards internationaux
pour papiers de création

国际标准的艺术纸

Internationale Standards
für Premiumpapiere

Conqueror
Curious Collection
Keaykolour
Opale
Pop'Set
Rives
Rives Sensation
Creative Labels

Arjowiggins Creative Papers
are distributed by Antalis

arjowigginscreativepapers.com

WELCOME

———

Something changes in us when we travel: Through exposure to new cultures and foreign contexts, we often return home filled with fresh perspectives that can make the everyday seem exotic. But worldly experiences don't start and end at the baggage claim, and it's what we do with those memories once we've unpacked our suitcases that really makes a difference in the long run. For The Travel Issue, we want to draw attention not only to far-flung locations but also to those who choose to stay local and see their surroundings anew.

Drawing upon our global community of contributors from Stockholm to Tokyo, we embarked on ventures in more than a dozen cities on four continents, such as jumping on a Soviet-era train in Hungary for a fashion shoot and sneaking behind the scenes with the tight-knit team at Hotel Fontevraud, which is housed in the stunningly refurbished interior of one of France's most famed abbeys.

We also visited two creative luminaries in their natural habitats: photographer and stylist Anita Calero, who after four decades in New York has decided to return home to her native Colombia, and musician Leon Bridges, who is bringing soul to the world (and the White House) without moving away from his Texan hometown of Fort Worth.

Some worldly entrepreneurs are lucky enough to be able to call arrival gates part of the job: The founder of fashion boutique Creatures of Comfort, the product designer behind Note Design Studio and the editors in chief of POPEYE, The Happy Reader and *Riposte* all share their trip tips and favorite locations both at home and abroad. We also spent a day with Justin Peck, the 28-year-old dancer who is the second-ever resident choreographer for New York City Ballet, as well as interviewing legendary essayist Pico Iyer and fashion designers Abdul Abasi of Abasi Rosborough and Ditte Reffstrup of Ganni.

While some thrill-seekers might have once competed over the number of monuments ticked off from an outdated Lonely Planet guidebook, many others now compete over the remoteness of the location. But at what point can our quest for "local experiences" alter the experience we set out to find in the first place? As well as an in-depth exploration into a generation's obsessive search for authenticity, we also chatted with a neuroscientist and a psychologist about how technologies such as virtual reality are changing the future of travel.

If all of this space-age talk makes you tired and hungry, then you're in luck: We've created a special room service–inspired menu that we encourage you to eat cross-legged on your bed while reading essays in this issue that discuss architect Le Corbusier's personal design pilgrimage, the surprising social rewards of choosing the middle seat and travel karma's ultimate comeuppance.

Travel is a mentality as much as an action, so it doesn't matter if our adventures start on the side of an alpine mountain or end in our living rooms. Simply getting out there and interacting with the world around us can be just as satisfying as any poolside retreat.

———

NATHAN WILLIAMS AND GEORGIA FRANCES KING

Starters

The Travel Issue

Tina Frey Designs
tinafreydesigns.com

tf

Starters

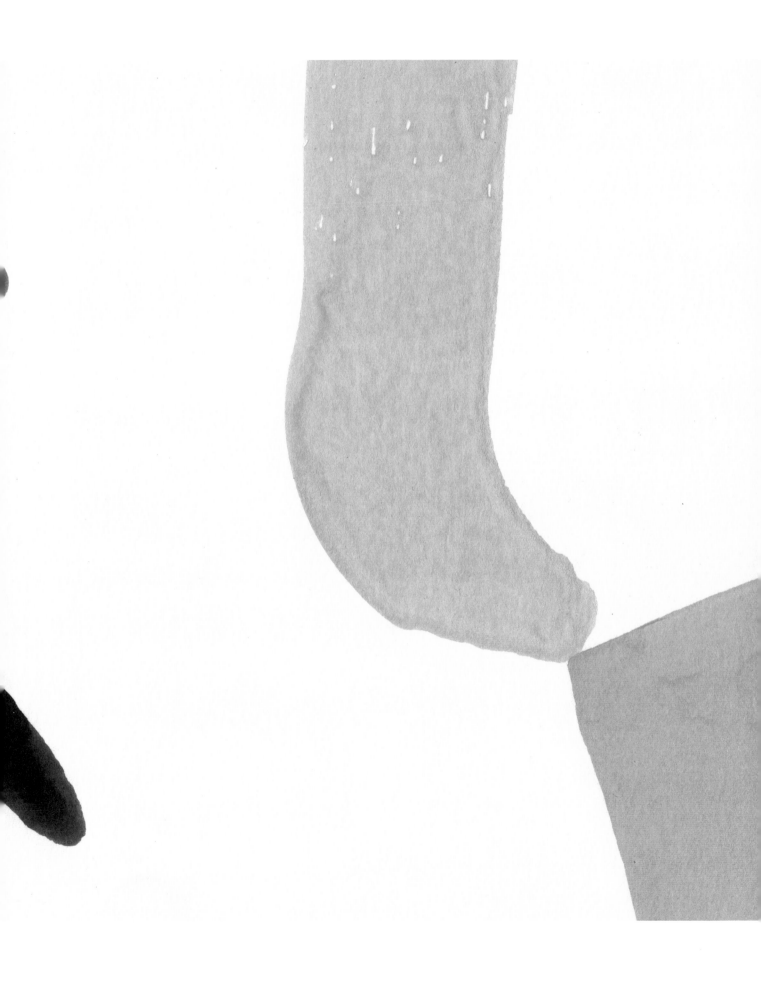

WORDS
KEITH FLANAGAN

Stuck in the Middle with You

It's said that the journey is more important than the destination, but what if that passage involves the utter decimation of your personal space at 35,000 feet?

Cross-continental adventurers often seek to cross borders that break comfort zones. But in order to reach those unknown horizons, we often must fly—and in uncomfortably tight circumstances that ironically limit the very freedom we chase.

Before we step off the plane and into a land of unlimited opportunity, we are first confined by a series of set, stagnant choices: beef or chicken, coffee or tea, peanuts or pretzels, aisle or window. Wedged between these seating options lies the most cited challenge a third of many economy passengers face: the middle seat.

Statistically, the middle seat is no man's land. According to polls by Skyscanner, only one percent of travelers choose the middle seat over the window or aisle. All three seats are physically uniform, measuring an average of 16.5 inches (42 centimeters) across. But psychologically, seats vary.

The anxiety of seat selection is a cognitive process in part explained by the study of proxemics: Our nervous systems help define our sense of personal space, and when that space is challenged, unruly behaviors manifest. The most familiar concept of proxemics is that of personal bubbles—those invisible zones around each person that, when breached, make us uneasy. "On airplanes, proxemics rules are broken," says Linda L. Nussbaumer, author of *Human Factors in the Built Environment*. "If individuals can select the seating where they are most comfortable, they may feel as if they have some control... however, not much."

In the tight confines of an aircraft, our normal proxemics rules are compressed because personal space is nearly nonexistent. For the passenger stuck in seat B, those in seats A and C are both just a little too close for comfort. Unable to escape, we make do by creating a sense of solitude among flanked strangers using silent cues: We lean away, turn our backs on our neighbors and brandish intellectual barriers constructed of *Wall Street Journals* and *New Yorkers*. We silence budding conversations with earbuds, scan new releases on embedded screens and avoid eye contact—anything and everything to ignore our neighbors.

How we seek comfort varies from passenger to passenger, and our seat choices are characteristic of our preferences. Having already sequestered themselves along a solid barrier, window-seat enthusiasts value privacy and enjoy a sense of limitless solitude that's only achieved by keeping their heads in the clouds. Passengers along the aisle lean toward freedom instead, moving through the cabin without needing permission and are the first to escape when the plane touches down.

But few would choose the middle seat of their own accord. Grazed by the adjacent bubbles of luckier neighbors, personal space is limited. Your movements are peripherally examined by the wingmen to your left and right: your screen visible, your page numbers notable, your breathing audible.

Nested by the window, passengers can soar. On the aisle, they can swan. Those in the middle? Cooped.

Before we spread our wings on the other side of the arrival gate, we hold tight to these waning moments of control—the seat assignment representing one of our last choices before uncertainty takes over. But perhaps that's the advantage of actually selecting seat B from the start: to willingly become the outlier even *before* we hit the baggage claim. Middle-seat sitters explore new terrains—and isn't that autonomy the reason that many of us travel in the first place? Since a plane ride is the ultimate limbo between here and there, why not embrace the adrenaline rush of the unknown even earlier in your expedition? Forget what you think you know; relinquish control; sit back, relax, and enjoy your flight.

After all, vacations don't commence at our destination: They begin as soon as we board the plane. And setting off on our journeys with open arms can allow us more than just enlightenment—it also earns us the right to both armrests.

WORDS
ADRIENNE MATEI

Dor

A nuanced hybrid of absence and nostalgia, dor conveys a loneliness you embrace, rather than overcome.

LANGUAGE: Romanian

PRONUNCIATION: "Dore" (rhymes with "more")

ETYMOLOGY: From the Latin *dolus*, which means "to ache"

MEANING: *Dor* refers to the feeling that seeps into your spirit when separated—either literally or figuratively—from your home and loved ones; it's a visceral, bittersweet yearning central to the shared Romanian cultural identity. Its genesis is related to both the melancholy of Romanian shepherds who spend months at a time alone away from home, as well as to the country's history of invasion, which required its inhabitants to periodically flee their native villages. Yet dor is not intended to be gloomy: Rather, it recalls the memory of cherished experiences, gives emotional significance to life and deepens your sense of social connectedness—a longing for the safety and contentment of a grandmother's kitchen.

USE: Dor is best used to anchor the oddly nourishing alienation you feel when estranged from the comforts of the past. Aside from its relation to homesickness, you might feel dor while rifling through old photographs or re-reading a favorite book.

WORDS
CARL HONORÉ

Doing the Time Warp

Resident slow living expert Carl Honoré explores the theory behind how time never stands still while on vacation.

Time flies when you're having fun. A really good party or a date with a new love interest almost always comes to an end too soon.

But there's a silver lining: Experiences that zoom by now often expand later in our memories—and that can make life feel longer. Nowhere is this more evident than when we travel. A great vacation whizzes past: You arrive, unpack, hit the sites—and next thing you know, it's time to go home. When you reminisce later though, the same vacation seems much longer.

This paradox is caused by our funky relationship with time itself. If the clock seems to spin faster when you're doing something new and interesting, it does the opposite when life gets routine and dull: Think how the minutes move like molasses when you're going through the motions at work.

Memory then plays further tricks on our internal metronomes: When we look back on our life, the boring patches barely register while the highlights loom large. In her book *Time Warped: Unlocking the Mysteries of Time Perception*, psychologist Claudia Hammond argues our memory of how long a period of time lasted has nothing to do with how quickly the minutes seemed to go at the time—it's how many novel and engaging experiences occurred during that period. The more memorable moments, the longer that time seems in retrospect.

If you do it right, travel is a feast of these moments. Hammond found when people look back on two weeks of their ordinary routine, they recall six to nine events on average. On vacation, we can rack up that many Kodak moments in a single day through eating unfamiliar food and meeting new people. By cranking up the novelty, a vacation passes swiftly at the time and then stretches out later in the memory.

Big minds have wrestled with this paradox. In his 1924 novel, *The Magic Mountain*, Thomas Mann probed into the ways that routine and novelty shape how we feel about the tempo and length of our lives. His warning against the peril of staying in your comfort zone was stark: "When one day is like all the others, then they are all like one; complete uniformity would make the longest life seem short."

So how can we use these insights to make life seem longer? Traveling more would help, but only up to a point: Mann also warned that novelty loses its tang after six to eight days away from home.

A simpler tactic is to recreate the thrill of travel by shaking up your normal routine to engineer more memorable moments: Changing your route to work might mean stumbling upon a magnolia tree in full blossom, or talking to a stranger could earn an invitation to an underground comedy club.

Time won't stop flying, but we can control the fun we have while it's soaring past. As the poet Cesare Pavese said, "We don't remember days, we remember moments."

NEW PERSPECTIVES ON SCANDINAVIAN DESIGN

MUUTO

New Nordic

WORDS
ANNE FULLERTON

A Wandering Mind

*More than physically transporting us
to a new place, travel takes the mind
into uncharted territory.*

At first glance, the cultural evidence that travel makes us more open, creative and curious seems irrefutable. From the Beat Generation's cross-country benders to Mark Twain's assertion that travel is "fatal to prejudice, bigotry, and narrow-mindedness," we assume without a second thought that seeing new places, people and cultures changes us for the better in ways that long outlast unflattering passport photos.

And yet for every adventure-hungry artist, there's a secluded genius who conjures a masterpiece using nothing more than their own limited experience and boundless imagination. Emily Brontë reinvented the Victorian novel and evoked vicious, vividly drawn relationships even though she lived most of her life in her picturesque family home. Likewise, Emily Dickinson—that other famously reclusive Emily—produced almost 1,800 poems over her lifetime despite leading such an isolated existence that she often spoke to visitors through her door and reportedly listened to her own father's funeral from the comfort of her bedroom. In the art world, postimpressionist painter Henri Rousseau is most famous for his jungle scenes—in spite of the fact that he never left France, let alone saw a jungle.

None of these creators strayed far from their garden paths, yet they all produced works as worthy of praise as their globe-wandering counterparts. So if we want to determine whether travel actually has any significant effect on creativity, we have to look beyond the typical narratives and personal anecdotes: And in recent years, that's exactly what psychologists and neuroscientists have been doing.

According to Paul Nussbaum, a psychologist and adjunct professor of neurological surgery at the University of Pittsburgh, it's not surprising that we feel more inspired when traveling. To start, travel *literally* changes our brains' structures. "Travel puts us into a novel and challenging situation we're not familiar with, so we're using our cortex," Nussbaum says. This activation causes our brain to sprout new dendrites, which are tiny branches on the brain cell that pull in information from the outside world. The more dendritic branches we grow, the more resilient our brains become.

While it's possible to grow dendrites in other ways, Nussbaum says that travel is ideal because it is—by definition—foreign. Rather than having to seek out novelty, we're immersed in a variety of unfamiliar stimuli all at once. "You're interacting with people who may not speak your language and might have a different code of dress, form of money, food and a totally different environment— all those things can be very beneficial for the brain," he says. "In order to survive, in some way, you're having to problem-solve. And that's what creativity really is: taking things you get exposed to and forming new ideas, solutions, products or services."

There is a wealth of quantitative research to support this view. Adam Galinsky, a professor at Columbia Business School, looked through 11 years of collections from hundreds of high-end fashion houses to see if there was a correlation between the creative directors' international experience and how innovative their designs were. As judged by independent buyers and journalists, he found that creative directors who had lived and worked in other countries produced more steadily inventive fashion lines for their brands than directors who had not. Why? Because "foreign experiences increase both cognitive flexibility and the ability to integrate information," he says. In other words, our brains become more adaptable and are better able to synthesize multiple viewpoints at once if they've been exposed to other cultures.

But there was a catch: According to Galinsky, traveling abroad did not reap the same benefits as living abroad. Though living in a greater number of countries increased creativity, it only did so up to a point—once a creative director had lived in three countries, the effects turned negative.

Galinsky and his team hypothesized that this all came down to one thing: how engaged we are with our surroundings. Moving frequently tends to make people less invested in their host city and, likewise, "Someone who lives abroad and doesn't engage with the local culture will likely get less of a creative boost than someone who travels abroad and really interacts with the local environment," Galinsky says. "The length of time spent in a place matters, but only because it increases the probability of deeper engagement."

So what does that mean for the average American, who takes only 11 vacation days a year? The good news is that we don't always need to go to another country to deeply engage with a new culture. "We have a tendency to self-segregate into groups of sameness—

ILLUSTRATION: KATRIN COETZER

to surround ourselves with people who think like us and look like us," says Joe O'Shea, the director of undergraduate research and academic engagement at Florida State University. In the same way that confirmation bias makes us more likely to believe information that supports our preexisting values, socializing with people who see the world in the same way as we do makes us feel safe and reassured. While this keeps us comfortable, "having homogeneous experiences and social networks dampens our cognitive and moral growth," O'Shea says. Even just breaking our routines to visit a different part of our own city or engaging with different kinds of people can have creative benefits.

Another way to make the most of your travels is to reflect on them afterward. Alina Black, principal designer at global design firm IDEO, is responsible for planning experiences locally and abroad to inspire and inform the company's design and strategy. According to her, making time to allow our minds to wander free from distraction is just as important as conscious reflection. "We design our experiences as much for serendipity and whimsy as we do for pointed research and expected outcomes," she says. "We want to allow for a variety of experiences but also for downtime. People really need that in order to soak in the learning and make space for things we couldn't have planned for."

As a person whose job involves both extensive travel and engineering inspiration on a daily basis, Black may have a unique perspective on the relationship between travel and creativity, but that doesn't mean she's immune to its challenges. In fact, she makes a point to mention something that the data often doesn't—that for all its benefits, travel can sometimes be bothersome. "Trying new things is not always enjoyable," Black says. "I hate to say this, but it's true. Sometimes, you do something and realize that there's a reason you don't do it on a regular basis—though that doesn't mean it's not helpful in that creative way."

Going in a new direction means we'll sometimes get lost, meeting new people means we won't like some of them, and seeing things from a different perspective means we have to question our own beliefs. But whether we're crossing a continent or walking home from a friend's house, it's worth remembering that the road less traveled is often also the more creative one.

PHOTOGRAPH: NICOLE FRANZEN

For Pico, adopting a traveler's mindset while staying rooted in your own city is all about intention. "Travel may facilitate openness—ideally opening eyes, and so minds and hearts and consciences—but it can't create it," he says. "You have to do the hard work of opening your mind and eyes yourself."

Pico Iyer

—

After a long trip, there is something to be said for making time to take stock of our experiences before jumping back into life. The acclaimed travel writer and author of The Art of Stillness explains how traveling the world can start with a simple step back.

Born to Indian academics, raised between the UK and the US and having lived in rural Japan with his Japanese wife for two decades, Pico Iyer is quite the globe-trotter in both his home and work life. As a regular essayist for *Time, The New York Times* and *Harper's* and the author of 10 books—ranging from *Video Night in Kathmandu* to *The Global Soul: Jet Lag, Shopping Malls, and the Search for Home*—Pico has seen the good, the bad and the ugly, ugly airport carpets. But it's not all foreign street signs and cultural immersion. Through spending much of his year hopping between countries, he has developed an appreciation for travel's opposite: stillness. We speak to Pico about his most surprising discoveries on the road and the upsides of belonging to a global community of nomadic world wanderers.

WHAT IS THE CONNECTION BETWEEN TRAVEL AND QUALITY OF LIFE?

The beauty of the global world is that you can get the same benefits of travel while at home or in the nearest big city. Your classroom or workplace is probably filled with people from Vietnam and India and Iran and Mexico, so you can now travel the globe just by walking down the street. In that regard, physically going around the world is less important than it ever was, except insofar as it takes you out of your comfort zone. But I'd say that travel can be a fine way to learn humility and how much you don't know.

OF ALL THE EXOTIC AND FAR-FLUNG PLACES YOU HAVE VISITED, WHICH HAS FELT THE MOST IMMEDIATELY LIKE HOME?

I've answered that with my feet by coming to live in Japan. Even when I was a little boy, I would only have to see a painting by Hiroshige in a museum or read a 10th-century Japanese poem to feel that I recognized them: They went through me with a piercing sense of familiarity that made me feel, "I know these places better than the house I grew up in or the place I live in now." So at the age of 29, I decided to pack up my things, quit my glamorous-seeming job in Midtown Manhattan, abandon my apartment on Park Avenue and move to a single room on the backstreets of Kyoto without its own toilet or telephone. It's the one decision I've never regretted. I believe that many of us have these secret homes—

faraway cultures with which we feel a strong affinity, even though we have no official connection with them. But the beauty of the present moment is that we can visit these places as never before and, if we're lucky, even make our homes in them. If my grandfather had felt a kinship with Japan, he might have been able to read about it in a book; in my father's generation, he might have been able to save up for a single visit. But nowadays, we can inhabit the place that makes the most sense to us and the one from which we most wish to learn. It's not a privilege I ever take for granted.

WHICH ELEMENT OF A CULTURE DO YOU FEEL BEST ENCAPSULATES IT, SUCH AS THE FOOD, DRESS, ARCHITECTURE OR LANGUAGE?

The body language, perhaps: I love sitting in a café and watching people walk past. Within seconds, just from the colors, the noises and the way groups form, you know whether you're in Italy, India, Bolivia or Japan—except that these days if you live in Toronto, San Francisco, London or Paris, many of the people walking past will be from Italy, India, Bolivia and Japan, importing their own sounds and rhythms into a fresh urban mix. Even home is much more exciting than it used to be.

WHAT HAS TRAVELING TAUGHT YOU ABOUT BALANCE?

Simply put, I have to be still in order to be moved. When I'm running around, I'm gathering materials such as experiences, emotions and visual stimuli, but to begin to make sense of them—to begin really to live with them—I have to be in one place, undistracted. I keep revisiting these trips, seeing them in new lights and finding new applications for them in my daily life. Travel lays the table for the feast you enjoy sitting still back home. Stillness is the end point of any trip; it's the way you convert sights into insights and bring the experience (in every sense) home.

WHAT CAN LIVING IN A DIFFERENT CULTURE TO THE ONE YOU'VE BEEN BROUGHT UP IN TEACH YOU ABOUT HOW THE WORLD WORKS AND YOUR PLACE IN IT?

I think living in a foreign place just shows you how there are no right answers and that everything you think you know is partial,

"When I'm running around, I'm gathering experiences and emotions, but to make sense of them, I have to be in one place. Travel lays the table for the feast you enjoy sitting still back home."

provisional and local. Sometimes when I'm at home—whether that home is in Japan or California—I begin to think I know what human life, reality and emotion all are. Then I'll mentally take myself back to North Korea, and within half an hour I'll see that everything I think of as universal and true doesn't begin to apply to people in these very different circumstances. My notions of the world are not just subjective, but fairly blind. Some people laugh at the North Koreans for not knowing much about how other cultures live, but I'm not sure we're much better. And we—unlike they—have no excuse for not knowing the world, given our relative freedom of movement and information.

YOU OFTEN SPEAK ABOUT ENJOYING FEELING LIKE AN OUTSIDER. WHAT FREEDOM DO YOU FEEL IT GIVES YOU?

On a very superficial level, the outsider enjoys all the benefits and beauties of a foreign culture without having to pay the taxes. Here in Japan, I can wander around like a perpetually enchanted—and bewildered—tourist without being subjected to the pressures and the often-paralyzing social responsibilities of my Japanese friends and neighbors. A traveler enjoys a makeshift kind of diplomatic immunity. But the deeper freedom, I hope, is that of not being stuck inside a particular perspective, or thinking that your way is the right way. I worry sometimes that in an age when we're lucky enough to have access to more cultures (and therefore more points of view and mind-sets) than ever, it's easier to surround yourself with people who think and look just like you. Being an outsider can protect you from that affliction.

HOW ARE OUR VIEWS OF DIFFERENT CULTURES CHANGING? ARE WE MOVING TOWARD BEING ONE MULTINATIONAL PEOPLE?

I think we are, whether we like it or not, if only because most people I know, especially in large cities in the affluent world, have friends, colleagues, neighbors and even spouses from radically different cultures. The number of people living in countries that are not their own already comes to over 230 million—four times

greater than the populations of Australia and Canada combined—and is increasing so quickly that in a few years there'll be more of us unplaceable souls than there are Americans. At the very least, we know a little more than we used to about other ways of thinking.

WHEN YOU WANT TO FEEL COMFORTED—THE *OPPOSITE* OF ADVENTUROUS—WHAT DO YOU ENJOY DOING?

I've always loved movies, and I will never say no to any sporting event, ever. In Japan, I often love turning out the lights while I'm waiting for my wife to come home and just listening to some music: soothing music sometimes, such as Bach, Leonard Cohen and Sigur Rós, but often not-so-soothing music, such as Green Day or The Clash. My ultimate comfort food, as you will have guessed already, is tea—my English upbringing and my Indian genes perhaps intensify that connection. Every year when my wife asks me what special treat I would like for my birthday, I give the worst and least generous answer possible: a plate of corn and a cup of tea. I can't help it; growing up in England in the 1960s and 1970s meant my taste buds were surgically extracted at birth. There, the equivalent of therapy, open-heart surgery and radiation are all known as "a cup of tea."

HOW HAS YOUR NOTION OF HOME CHANGED OVER TIME?

I think my notion of home—as a collage, a work-in-progress, a stained-glass whole made up of all the many places that have formed me—has been pretty much the same all my life. What made this clear to me with particular vibrancy was when my family home in California burned down in a forest fire, and I lost every last thing that I owned. That showed me, unquestionably, that whatever sense of home I had would have to be portable, invisible, internal. The only home that could sustain me would be whatever I carried around with me, whatever my circumstances—my friendships, my values and my passions.

Pico Iyer's latest book is The Man Within My Head *(Vintage, 2013).*

SPRING 2016
AGJEANS.COM

WORDS
JOHN CLIFFORD BURNS

Travel Karma

*When swept up in travel's romantic haze,
we sometimes forget to leave a place better—
and not worse off—than the way we found it.*

In search of travel enlightenment, we often forget about travel karma. When we depart from our sojourns, we take memories and souvenirs with us, but rarely do we think about what we leave behind—an unmade bed at an apartment rental, a broken heart in Europe or a phone on the backseat of a taxi. Traveling can alter the mind, but what we alter doesn't often cross that same mind.

In modern times, the Boy Scouts tell us to leave the campsite in a better state than how we found it. But mythical wayfarers of the past also show us how to act. For example, the ancient Norse god Odin lived in the city of Asgard. Despite it being lovely, by all accounts, Odin yearned for something more, so he packed some sensible travel essentials (including a wide-brimmed hat and a sturdy knapsack) and kissed Asgard goodbye in pursuit of greener grass and worldly wisdom.

Fortunately for him, the location of that oft searched-for wisdom had exact coordinates in Norse mythology: at Mimir's Well, near an old tree called Yggdrasil. In order to gain something valuable from the world, Odin realized he needed to give something equally dear in return. The story goes that he volunteered his right eye in bloody exchange for the wisdom he took—but we don't have to gouge our eyes out for good travel karma (even if we may occasionally feel like doing so while waiting to claim our baggage at the airport).

Instead, we can simply open our eyes to see what we can bring to a new city beyond our suitcases. By doing this, we can consider not only what we leave behind, but how much we're taking in the first place.

Stopping to lend someone your jumper cables or helping change a flat tire can earn you some ↓ quick and easy travel karma.

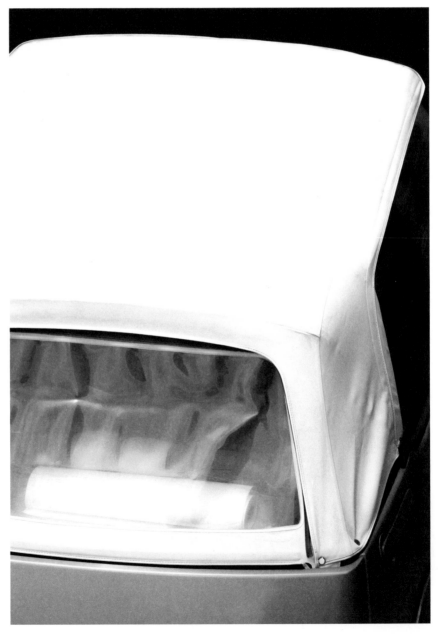

PHOTOGRAPH: FREDERIK VERCRUYSSE

Laurent *by* &LAMBERT FILS studio

WORDS
DUSTIN COSENTINO

Field Notes:
Le Corbusier

From grappling with the effects of the Industrial Revolution to reveling in awe at the beauty of the Parthenon, Le Corbusier's early travels had a lasting influence on his iconic 20th-century architecture.

The early travels of architect, urban planner, artist and all-around Renaissance man Le Corbusier were highly influential on both his later work and his philosophy of how to live. What began as reconnaissance turned into a lifelong obsession as he crisscrossed the globe, studying and executing ideas on how to set the great advances of modern civilization against their calamitous repercussions on society. Today, we can travel from France to India and back again to see the outcome of his experiments, but to better understand his intentions, it's best to look back on his first sojourns.

Born Charles-Édouard Jeanneret-Gris in 1887 and raised in the small Swiss town of La Chaux-de-Fonds in the Jura mountains, Le Corbusier came from a family of watchmakers and musicians. Feeling confined by the tiny, conservative town of his youth, young Charles-Édouard read widely and escaped as soon as he could, first to Italy and then to Eastern Europe. The latter journey, which he undertook in 1911 at the impressionable age of 24, saw him traverse a route that led from Berlin to Prague, down the Danube past Vienna, through the Balkans, onward to Istanbul, then to Athens and back via Pompeii and Rome.

Armed with a notebook, camera and binoculars, it was during this period that Charles-Édouard, who later adopted the byname Le Corbusier, became fixated on deciphering the world that had formed in the aftermath of the Industrial Revolution. This era was pockmarked with upheavals and was on the brink of social collapse with urban centers such as Paris and Berlin struggling with rapid expansion and the development of slums. The craft-based value system on which society had been running for so long was crumbling—a fact that wasn't lost on the citizens of Le Corbusier's hometown, which specialized in only one industry: watches. In essence, his travels became a search for origin and meaning in a world increasingly without either.

In *Voyage d'Orient*—as the published account of his early venture has now come to be known—Le Corbusier wrote and drew a great deal, depicting both the landscapes he saw and the people

LEFT PHOTOGRAPH: ÅKE E:SON LINDMAN; RIGHT PHOTOGRAPH: HELENA ARIZA

The Couvent Sainte-Marie de La Tourette is a monastery of the Dominican order in Éveux, France. Composed of reinforced concrete, the structure was Le Corbusier's last major project in Europe and comprises 100 individual cells, a church, a rooftop cloister, classrooms and a communal library.

who lived within them. But more than anything, he studied buildings: He spent six weeks in Athens alone, studying and drawing the Parthenon, a building that he described as a *machine à émouvoir* (an "emotion-arousing machine") and later juxtaposed with his famous declaration that a house is a *machine à habiter* (a "machine for living").

He also studied the geometry of buildings and how light and space were used to their utmost advantage: Through numerous drawings and descriptions, he recreated the awe-inspiring lighting effect under the massive dome of Hagia Sophia in Istanbul, which is produced by rows of windows encircling its base. The enduring impact of this memory can still be clearly seen in a number of his buildings, including one of his last designs for a church at Firminy in central France.

In addition to experiencing the colossal ambition of immense structures such as these, his work owes an equal amount to the folk architecture he encountered along the way. He especially noted the ubiquitous whitewash material employed on the exteriors of buildings by rich and poor alike, which he praised for its economy and versatility. The influence of this observation reaches from his early white buildings such as the Villa Savoye and his famous chapel at Ronchamp all the way to his use of raw concrete in his later Brutalist architecture.

Despite Le Corbusier's early cultural exposure and progressive attitude, his politics were a mixed bag. For example, in the 1920s, he strongly advocated demolishing downtown Paris to make way for a series of towering skyscrapers. In the early 1930s, he submitted a design for the Palace of the Soviets in Moscow, which was to be built on the rubble of a 19th-century cathedral destroyed by Stalin. And during World War II, he was on a planning committee with the puppet Vichy government of German-occupied France while also acting as a technical adviser for a eugenics foundation.

But these morally problematic viewpoints also gave way to a more enlightened outlook. Witnessing the large, unprecedented displacement of populations after World War I (and even more so after World War II) only strengthened Le Corbusier's desire to build for as many people as possible. Whether this was for workers at the Weissenhof estate in Stuttgart, for families at the polychrome Unité d'Habitation in Marseille or for the Dominican monks at La Tourette outside Lyon (pictured previous spread), his core motive was always to fuse what he felt was good about the new with what was tried-and-true from the past. Thankfully, only his more honorable investigations have stood the test of time.

Le Corbusier died of a heart attack in 1965 while swimming in the ocean, 55 years after writing *Voyage d'Orient* and a year before it was first published. His buildings have since become pilgrimage sites in their own right, inspiring subsequent generations—sketchbooks in hand—to experience them directly and formulate their own visual culture.

As Le Corbusier wrote not long before his death, "Others stood indifferent—but you saw!"

PILGRIMAGE POINTS

Hôtel Le Corbusier, Marseille, France
Check in here to experience part of Unité d'Habitation—a residential complex demonstrating the architect's utopian ambitions.

National Museum of Western Art, Tokyo, Japan
Hosting a collection of impressionist art, this boxy building in Ueno Park is one of the architect's three museums to make it off of paper.

Chandigarh, India
An entire city designed and planned by Le Corbusier, Chandigarh still runs on his bold ideas on modernism and social experimentation.

Couvent Sainte-Marie de La Tourette, Éveux, France (previous spread)
The last of the architect's major works in France, this modernist Dominican monastery can also be rented out for retreats and professional seminars.

Carpenter Center for the Visual Arts, Cambridge, Massachusetts
Located among the red bricks of Harvard University, this center dedicated to art and design is Le Corbusier's only building in the US.

Tombe de Le Corbusier, Roquebrune-Cap-Martin, France
Overlooking the Mediterranean sea, the headstone that Le Corbusier designed for himself captures his belief in nature and geometry's beauty.

INTERVIEW
TAYLOR WEIK

Arthur Groeneveld

————

During the years he spent living between Amsterdam and Berlin, Arthur Groeneveld amassed dozens of interests he couldn't narrow down—so he pursued them all.

Originally from a small coastal town in the Netherlands, Arthur Groeneveld started as a one-man show with his first company, A Guy Named Arturo. He then co-founded the creative consulting collective 1kg before he and his partner in business and life, Bamboo van Kampen, began working with clients ranging from boutique hotels to publications through their agency, Arturo Bamboo. While working with such diverse businesses, institutions and individuals might seem overwhelming, Arthur has learned to allow the stress to extend and not shrink his creative boundaries.

YOU JUMP BETWEEN A LOT OF DIFFERENT MEDIUMS. HOW DOES THIS BREATHE LIFE INTO YOUR WORK?

This diversity along with its many spillover effects is what makes my work so absorbing. At one point I realized that you only have one life—it's short and work makes up such a big part of it—so it better be fulfilling! Each project, market and client is very different, and this makes the work interesting.

HOW IS DOING CONSULTING WORK FOR A FASHION BRAND DIFFERENT FROM WORKING WITH AN ART OR ARCHITECTURAL COMPANY?

The art world is an amazing but difficult environment to work in: It has a unique, potent voice that can amaze, surprise, shock, teach and stun. Art's language is universal, and museums and galleries have the power to get you out of your daily routine and make you see things differently. Architecture is a completely separate realm where so much comes together—it's like dressing the world to be ready for the future. And when working with fashion, I automatically connect the brand to other creative disciplines and create something real and human, which are two values that can be absent in this fast-paced world.

HOW DO YOU CHANNEL YOUR FEARS INTO CREATIVE ENERGY?

Adrenaline is what keeps me going. Sometimes a stressful moment pushes me to the next level and another state of mind where special things can happen. When a project is coming together really nicely, I feel a different kind of energy—an exciting one. It's all about keeping these different forms of adrenaline in balance.

DO YOU THINK THAT BEING A "JACK-OF-ALL-TRADES, MASTER OF NONE" IS THE FUTURE FOR CREATIVES?

Of course "knowing a little about a lot" has certain limitations, but to me, it's not a bad thing. The new generation seems to go through 10 different jobs in 10 years rather than just staying in one job for 10 years, and this development shows a certain shift in society. It's not about safety and money in the long term; it's about life here and now, learning new skills and pushing your own boundaries.

PLEASE TELL US ABOUT YOUR HOME.

I live in a cozy Altbau apartment in Berlin-Neukölln with my girlfriend, Bamboo. It's my favorite area in Berlin: It's next to the airport-turned-public park, Tempelhof, and has lots of cafés, stores and a great weekly market. When we moved, our home had just been renovated with ceiling ornaments, perfect white walls and simple wooden flooring. In order to maintain creative space for ideas and projects in our heads, we try to keep our house minimal yet warm with a combination of pieces inherited from Bamboo's great-grandmother, art from friends and newer furniture.

WHAT DO YOU LIKE TO DO TO UNWIND?

To completely relax and slow down, Bamboo and I spend time in nature. Whether it's at the seaside or in the snow, I'm always completely stunned by the power, space and silence of nature. You tend to forget this while living in a city, and I feel more and more attracted to it. Simple pleasures such as reading books, painting, watching films, enjoying food and wine with friends and visiting exhibitions and museums also relax me.

WHEN NOT WORKING, WHAT DO YOU DO IN YOUR PERSONAL TIME TO SPARK INSPIRATION?

One of my biggest passions is traveling: Getting to know new cultures and being inspired by people is the most incredible energizer. Jogging along the sea or going snowboarding works like meditation and gives me space in my head—the best ideas come during these sessions. It's amazing to be active, out in nature and to have this certain feeling of freedom.

Arthur wears jeans by
American Apparel and
a vintage sweater

Ditte Reffstrup

———

As the creative force behind Danish brand
Ganni, this designer's collections reflect
her favorite pair of sneakers—comfortable
and great on the dance floor.

Raised in the rural town of Hirtshals in Denmark, Ditte Reffstrup used to get her teenage fashion fix glued to MTV or trawling local charity shops. Now as the creative director of Ganni, her own Copenhagen-based fashion line, Ditte finds herself looking for inspiration as far afield as Los Angeles and Tokyo. Despite winning awards and having her designs stocked in more than 20 countries around the world, she says her brand can best be described in much the same way as her kitchen: "Scandinavian in style, but a little messy."

CAN YOU REMEMBER THE MOMENT YOU REALIZED YOU WANTED TO BE A FASHION DESIGNER?
There wasn't one person or thing—it's just always been a part of my life. When I was in kindergarten, I'd crawl under the bed screaming if my mom wanted to put a pair of overalls on me! I was really determined in what I wanted to wear, but I thought it was natural and that everyone felt like that. So becoming a designer was more of an instinct or a feeling.

WHAT WAS IT LIKE GROWING UP AS A BUDDING DESIGNER IN PROVINCIAL DENMARK?
I was a dreamer. When you're from a small town, it's not always popular to be different, and I was. I was very much alone, but that wasn't a problem—actually, I preferred it.

IF WE LOOKED IN YOUR WARDROBE, WOULD WE FIND ANYTHING SURPRISING?
I have a pair of Skechers that I bought for five bucks in LA many years ago—old people in Miami and LA wear them, but I think they're so cool. I had a pair of soccer boots too—I used to play soccer from the age of five to 18. That was the thing I had going back in my hometown... playing with the bad girls at the soccer club. That was me.

WHERE DO YOU LOOK FOR INSPIRATION NOW?
I'm lucky that I have a job where I get to travel a lot. Last spring I went to Tokyo for the first time. It was so beautiful and so different, so pure and light. It fused the classic culture—the old prints and the kimonos and the way of serving tea—with the young people who are so crazy-looking! Those two aesthetics combined were really inspiring.

WHAT DO YOU AND YOUR HUSBAND, NICOLAJ (THE CEO OF GANNI), HAVE IN COMMON?
We're both from the countryside, which I actually hated most of my life! I always thought, "If I had just grown up in Copenhagen, things would've been so much easier." But the older I get, the more I feel that it was really good that I grew up where I did—that's why I'm where I am now. Ganni has become bigger, so the work has become bigger. And when it becomes bigger, there's more pressure; sometimes it's easier to be an underdog that nobody was expecting. If I get really stressed, I just want to go home.

WHAT DO YOU DO IN YOUR FREE TIME TO RELIEVE THAT TENSION?
I wish I could tell you that I was still sporty! I specifically wish that I were the type of person who plays tennis or runs—but I'm not. I know it's important for your physical health, and I've tried everything, but I think it's so boring. My sport is dancing, on Saturday nights!

Ditte wears
a sweater, shirt
and trousers
by Ganni and
sneakers by Nike

Abdul wears a
shirt, jacket and
trousers by Abasi
Rosborough

AS TOLD TO
JOHN CLIFFORD BURNS

Abdul Abasi

*From front line to front row: New York-
based fashion designer Abdul Abasi shares
how his military background guides his
brand's futuristic approach to menswear.*

PHOTOGRAPH: NICOLE FRANZEN

Inspiration can sometimes hit at the most unexpected moments. While stationed in the Netherlands with the US Army in his early 20s, fashion designer Abdul Abasi came to love the vibrant design and street style he saw during off-duty rambles around Amsterdam. In 2006, he traded his position as a NATO missile technician for a place at New York's Fashion Institute of Technology (FIT), and there he met classmate Greg Rosborough, who would later become his business partner. Now three years into his role as creative director of the duo's own line, Abasi Rosborough, Abdul shares how his own ethos and the brand's mission to modernize menswear is rooted in his military past.

Fashion is communication. Whether you're a politician, a soldier or a chef, whatever you wear communicates an idea and speaks to a certain tribe or social construct you want to be a part of.

I was in the US military before moving to New York. One of the beautiful things about the military was that I got to travel a lot—I lived in the Netherlands, Korea and Germany—and was able to explore cities and see different cultures. On the clock, the military is about conformity and working together for a common goal, but as soon as you take off the uniform and get out and about, you're just like any other civilian: And you want to look presentable in normal clothes.

I was stationed in the Netherlands for more than three years, and that's where I picked up the bug for fashion. I really saw menswear there in a new light—in an artistic, irreverent sort of space, rather than just as a commercially driven idea.

The first real garment I designed and constructed was with the help of a bunch of middle-aged Dutch women. I had picked up a sewing machine in a local shop and had seen an ad for a sewing circle, so I used to drive into the countryside to sit with the women and learn how to sew. After attending a few classes, I drew a sort of cropped trench coat, and the woman heading the group helped me design it. I was so proud of it that when I went to my admissions interview at FIT, I brought that piece with me. It impressed the head of the menswear department, and he accepted me.

I graduated from FIT in 2008. I met Greg there, but it's ironic, because we weren't the best of friends in school—I was a little older, and I may have been a bit more of a loner. Out of school, both Greg and I were working for other designers. Although the experience was great, we both felt stifled by the fact that every time we wanted to design something, we had to look into an archive—to look at what had previously been done and reinterpret it.

Years later, we reconnected to tackle the idea of modernizing the men's wardrobe. Greg and I are two sides of the same coin: He's very pragmatic, a great leader, very organized and detail-oriented, whereas I'm a bit more spatial, intuitive and use abstract thinking.

> "Intuition is such an important part of our lives. It's about your gut feeling: I don't do anything I feel is unequivocally wrong or counter to my personality or my values."

When someone works with me, I want them to know that I take a holistic approach to everything. I think intuition is such an important part of our lives. It's about your gut feeling: I don't do anything I feel is unequivocally wrong or counter to my personality or my values. For example, Greg and I have certain dogmas behind our design ethos, and one of them is using natural fiber: We're big proponents of using sustainable fabrics that are natural and biodegradable. Now we're just trying to figure out how to integrate that with design items that are emotional and soulful.

In any sort of creative endeavor, it's always good to have someone to challenge your ideas. Through defending our ideas, Greg and I are able to come up with the purest and strongest products. We really support each other and balance one another out. Fashion is a very tough industry, so it's also good to have someone around who has your back—someone who supports you, has put in the same amount of work and sacrifice as you have and is willing to share the labor. We've sacrificed a lot to create our own business, and we've done things that many people have refused to do or are not able to do. I think that comes from my time in the military: The discipline and the attention to detail have served me well in fashion.

The military is also the biggest fashion reference ever, without a doubt: It never goes out of style. Every menswear garment is a derivative of it. I love the beauty of military design because function is paramount. In the military, I wasn't so conditioned to look at that, but it has definitely subliminally seeped into the way I think. Abasi Rosborough is not overtly military in any respect, but it operates under the same principle: function first.

I'm very big into the ideology and theory behind design—the reasons we make things and why those things are well designed or not. I'm a student of design history; I enjoy researching da Vinci, the Bauhaus movement, Jean Prouvé and all those polymaths. What I love about the era preceding ours is that if you were a designer, you designed buildings as well as furniture—there was no categorization or specialization. You knew design through and through, and you could design anything.

Growing up, I felt like I could do anything that I wanted to do—I really didn't feel limited by my race, gender or culture. My parents are Nigerian immigrants; they moved to the States around 40 years ago, and I was their first child born here. Typically, first-generation immigrants are kind of torn between two cultures: You have your mother tongue and your mother culture, and then you're thrust into a totally different setting. But I was growing up in a very diverse neighborhood and didn't have a sense of my race being lesser than anyone else's. I think that allows me to navigate between different cultures now.

Today I live in Jackson Heights, Queens. It's extremely diverse: There are more than 200 languages spoken in this area, and there are lots of restaurants that serve food from South India, Thailand, Tibet and Bengal. Greg lives in Brooklyn, where we also have our studio, and we make all our clothes in Manhattan's Garment District. I'm in love with New York: So many things are possible here. For example, the fact that we can design and manufacture a collection in one city is quite amazing.

I love to go to the different galleries in Chelsea to see exhibitions—I find inspiration in art and in the processes that artists have, and I really try to utilize that in our fashion practice. Too many designers reference other fashion designers, and I don't think you can bring anything new to the table that way. But if you can look at different processes—whether it's those of sculptor Richard Serra or artist Douglas Wheeler—you can use the same sort of logic but implement it in a different context. There's something fresh when you do that; art is an everlasting well of inspiration.

In the three years we've been running Abasi Rosborough, Greg and I have learned that we have to balance familiar items and emotional responses with design, forward-thinking and function. I think we're at a good place now, and we've definitely developed our own handwriting.

Above: Abdul is pictured outside the Stephen A. Schwarzman Building of the New York Public Library, which was designed by architects John Merven Carrère and Thomas Hastings and is located next to Bryant Park in Manhattan's bustling Midtown district.

Travel

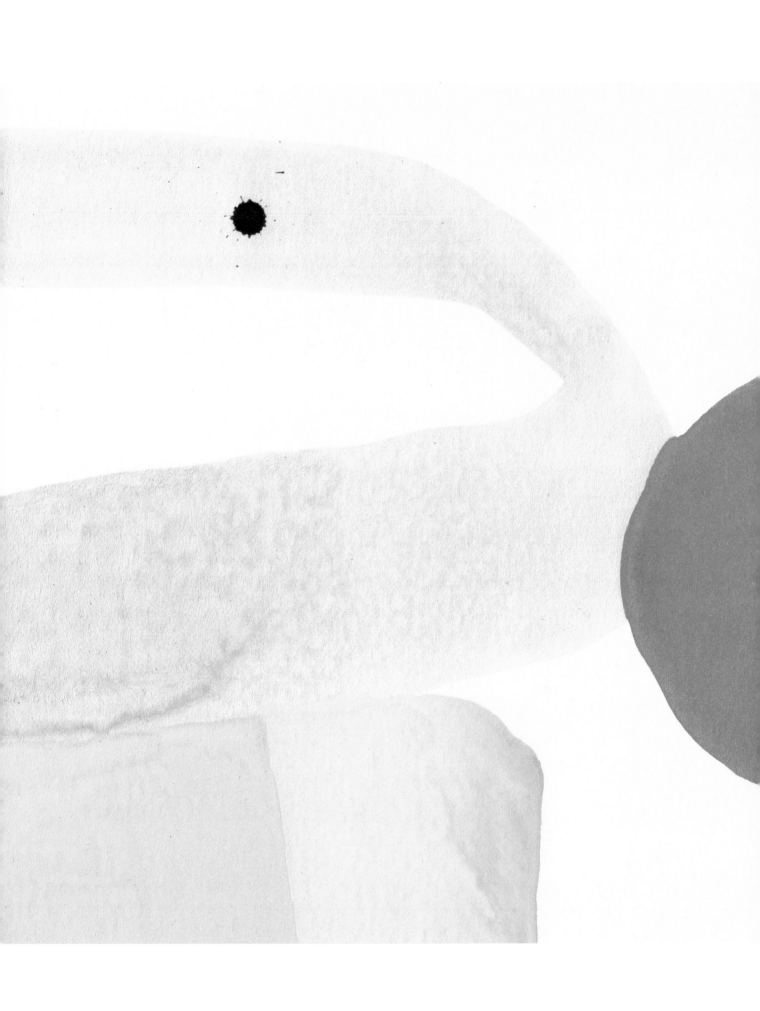

WORDS
DIANA BUDDS

PHOTOGRAPHS
STEFAN HEINRICHS

STYLING
ALPHA VOMERO

During her years as a prop stylist and photographer in New York, Anita Calero honed a knack for spotting perfection in the imperfect and discerning elegance in the everyday. Whether it was in the outfits she constructed to go dancing at Studio 54 or in the shoots she did for some of the biggest magazines of the '80s, Anita pushed the boundaries of her own creativity. Now, after four decades, she is following the call back home to her native Colombia.

The Naturalist
Anita Calero

In order to capture life in photographs, you need to have lived it first. From making ends meet chauffeuring Greek royalty in a gold Cadillac during her younger years to shooting some of the world's biggest brands in her later decades, photographer and stylist Anita Calero has certainly made her time count. Though she is best known for capturing sublime still lifes, her reputation as an artist is often preceded by her presence as a woman—she exudes effervescence and graciousness, and she possesses an invigorating aura that belies her years. At 63, Anita is now embarking on the next chapter of her personal narrative: a homecoming of sorts to her native Cali, Colombia.

After almost four decades spent living and working in New York, Anita recently sold nearly all her possessions and decamped from the frenetic city to a simpler place where her family takes priority. "I had friends, colleagues and great art directors in New York, but family was missing," she says. "I think my life was meant to end up in Colombia." Though a brief flirtation with retirement ignited the shift in her mind-set, this move is less about grinding to a screeching halt and more about adopting balance.

During her years in America, Anita became known for her prop styling and photography work, which runs the gamut from interiors to food spreads and product shoots. "I don't like monotony," she says. "In the studio, outside of the studio, I like the variety." Regardless of her client or subject matter, Anita makes what's opposite her lens truly shine: A freshly butchered pork chop looks as sumptuous as an Italian leather handbag; a sweatshirt from UNIQLO as exalted as linens from Missoni. "I want to bring the beauty out of the mundane," she says. "I always compose scenes to give objects a life of their own."

Anita's knack for coaxing elegance from the everyday started at an early age. The second youngest of six children, she grew up in a creative household and found solace on her family's farm in Colombia amid the vast fields, open skies and spirited horses. This stoked her love of the natural world—a through-line in her life. "I was always enamored with nature," she says. "I'd climb trees and stay out there for hours. I was fascinated with the wind and the way trees moved." Her father, an MIT-educated civil engineer, had a business importing motors, which often arrived in wood crates. Instead of throwing them out, her mother saw potential in the wood and saved them to build custom furniture for the house. Her parents' resourcefulness and ability to perceive something beyond its prescribed value came to inform how Anita herself viewed the world: that the right eye can elicit beauty in the unexpected.

During her teenage years, Anita went through a freewheeling streak—one that arguably continued into her adult life. She never hewed to the rigid structure of a classroom, preferring and yearning for more freedom instead. "I wasn't a good student, meaning I had a lot of art in me," she quips. After she received a few failing grades, Anita's parents decided to send her abroad. At 15 she embarked on a two-year stint in Switzerland to learn French

Anita Calero

"They invented egos in photography. I said to myself, 'Make sure when you enter this field that you don't copy that attitude, because it's not a healthy one.'"

Anita Calero

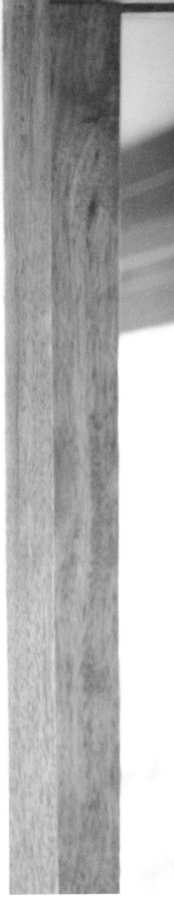

Anita Calero

("Switzerland taught me organization, which I love," she says. "It goes with my Virgo personality"), then she went on to live in England for a year. Coming of age in Europe during the '60s and '70s exposed her to a range of cultural experiences that she might not have encountered otherwise. "I wouldn't say that I was rebellious: I was curious," she says. "I was both a hippie and a punk—I went with whatever the movement was. But I wasn't a true punk that pierced their nose or got tattooed—I picked up the nice sides of everything. Instead of being consumed by it, I took the slight beauty of it all. It was a freedom of expression."

Leaving Colombia—and the constraints she felt from the traditional family structure—offered Anita the chance to discover who she was on her own terms: someone who was curious, free-spirited and intent on exploring new experiences. "I knew what I wanted from day one, and I went for it," she says. "Whatever I wanted, I did. I wasn't shy or coy about going forward in my life." Though Anita has forged ahead steadily with her own intense focus, she also describes her life thus far as a series of fortuitous meetings and opportunities—a fated journey of sorts. Many of the pivotal leaps of her 20s went on to have an indelible effect on her personal and professional path.

It began in her early 20s when Anita moved to Miami, Florida, after meeting and then marrying her husband, Javier Rodriguez. She and Javier were shopping for sheets (intended to be a wedding present from her parents) at a local department store when she was served by a fellow young expat: Maria Robledo, who would go on to become a renowned photographer—and Anita's partner of 18 years. Months later, after a series of near-misses—"she had a boyfriend, I was married, life went on," Anita says—Maria happened to be living in an apartment only blocks away from the home Anita shared with her husband. It was there that their friendship, relationship and professional careers all developed in the darkroom built into Anita's home.

"She was in college to become an architect, and I was a photographer," Anita recalls. "My husband had built a darkroom in the house and she was very curious about photography. I was the one who put a camera in her hand—I opened her up, and now she's the greatest photographer! We became friends, and then we fell in love with each other."

In 1977, at the age of 25, Anita left her husband and moved to New York to be with Maria, who had been accepted into the School of Visual Arts. After going back and forth between Miami

and New York for some time, the allure of the downtown creative scene eventually won her over: the fiercely independent artists, the freedom of expression, the camaraderie and, of course, the famous social scene. "I went to the school of Studio 54," she jokes of the famed disco-era nightclub. "It was hard to get into: You'd wait in the crowd for a long time. They knew who to pick to come in—you had to have the look, because if you didn't have the little outfit that brought the circus inside, you weren't welcome."

Maria's brother, the designer Roberto Robledo, would create custom outfits for the whole crew—"the pirate look, the gypsy look," she lists—that allowed them to explore the outer edges of their personas together. "We were all very artistic and free," Anita says of her friends at the time, who included the likes of avant-garde opera singer Klaus Nomi and fashion designer Anna Sui. "We created our own looks or would go to thrift stores and find things to wear. Our guts spoke to our designs—we weren't influenced by anything. It was a happy time with dancing, discos and clubs."

Roberto contributed to more than just her outlandish fashion choices: With his help, Anita landed a job as a salesperson at Patricia Field, the storied fashion destination that, while now closed, remains revered to this day. Field is a costume designer who won an Emmy Award for her work on *Sex and the City*, and her store attracted cultural icons such as Patti Smith, Debbie Harry and, more recently, Lady Gaga, Missy Elliott and Miley Cyrus. Back in the '70s, art luminary Jean-Michel Basquiat was a regular customer—he even once painted one of the store's disposable paper jumpsuits for Anita. If she'd chosen to keep the garment as a memento of the time, it could've been worth hundreds of thousands of dollars in today's art market, but money was never the point. "We all connected and treated each other like artists," she says of her associates during this era. "We did art, but it wasn't like it was going to end up at Christie's."

Anita's casual attitude toward fame and her guileless countenance drew attention from the right people, which led her to a further succession of chance meetings, acquaintances and jobs. For example, through her connections at Patricia Field, Anita became a chauffeur for Prince Michael of Greece. "The car was a fascinating chapter!" she says. "He thought it was so fun to have this young girl driving a gold Cadillac Eldorado." Dressed in her self-made uniform, complete with real jockey boots, she would ferry the prince and his artist wife from party to party. Thanks to him and his revelries, to which she was sometimes invited, she was able to rub elbows with the city's elite.

"It's about being in the right place and having some kind of a guardian angel," Anita says of her fated run-ins. "I don't know what it is—just some kind of luck."

A little good fortune and a lot of unbridled talent soon saw Anita's creative career start to swell. At this time, Maria was working as an assistant for a photographer whose girlfriend was Paula Greif, an art director at *Mademoiselle*. Paula noticed Anita's work and invited her to be her assistant, and it wasn't long before she began

---

Previous spread: When constructing her home in Colombia, Anita prioritized reconnecting with the natural surroundings that were an integral aspect of her childhood. Her house is situated in the middle of a forest, and Anita often keeps the doors and windows open to allow the birds, butterflies and iguanas that wander around her garden to come indoors.
Left: Anita wears a dress by Apiece Apart. On pages 50 and 68, she wears her own clothes. On pages 55 and 63, she wears a shirt by Studio Nicholson and jeans by Levi's. On page 66, she wears a shirt by COMME des GARÇONS. She wears her own jewelry throughout.

styling shoots for Gael Towey, the influential creative director who helped launch *Martha Stewart Living*, and Mary Shanahan, an art director whose career spanned from *Rolling Stone* to French *Vogue*. "Mary encouraged me to go for that dream," Anita says. "She was the ideal art director, trusting us and giving us confidence."

It was only a matter of time before Anita and Maria began working together professionally as an "us": Anita would style the shoots and set up the angles, and then Maria would take over for the actual shutter clicking and technical photographic production. The two became renowned in the publishing world for their creative collaborations, forming what she says became known in inner circles as "The Maria and Anita Look." But after 18 years, their professional and romantic relationship ended. "When we broke up people said, 'Why? You guys were an institution!'" she says. Once enough time had passed, Gael encouraged Anita to get behind the camera again and transition from being a prop stylist into a professional photographer. It was the push that Anita needed. "Gael said, 'When you're ready to show your work, I want to give you your first job,'" she says.

However, Anita was wary about getting back behind the lens, as the technical part of photography didn't interest her as much as building the composition. To re-learn the mechanics, she hired an assistant who showed her how to use a 4x5 camera properly and traveled to the south of France for the summer, where a friend had rented a château and had invited her to stay. Anita built a makeshift studio in a crumbling corner of the estate, shopped at the farmers markets for flowers and fruit and began composing still lifes. After a couple of hiccups, she finally achieved a photograph that she believed transcended all those she'd produced before it.

"It came out, and it was like having a baby," Anita says. "I ran through the château to show an art director who was staying with us. I said, 'Look, my first photograph!' And she said, 'Whatever you're doing, do it again.' From then on, history." When she returned to the States, Anita assembled her portfolio and presented it to Gael. "That day I ended up with three jobs," she says.

In the decades that have passed since Anita stepped into her first darkroom, attitudes in the trade have changed. "I think they invented egos in photography," she says. "I said to myself, 'Make sure when you enter this field that you don't copy that attitude, because it's not a healthy one.' So I don't allow myself to go that route." Moreover, the industry had continued to evolve through dramatic shifts in image-making and technology, especially the move from film to digital photography. Though she uses the latter today, Anita reminisces about composing stills for her 4x5 camera—the large-format device favored by Alfred Stieglitz, Edward Weston and Tina Modotti. "I miss my film, I miss my old world—it was more intimate," she says. "Now you just deal with the computer. I'd much rather have my film back. The sound of my Polaroid when it opened—that is one thing I'll never forget."

Anita's photography mirrors the interior worlds in which she resides. Both are studies in contrasts—a medley of colors, textures

Anita Calero

"Coming back to Colombia is what I needed. I missed my roots, my soil, my birds, my smells, my fruit, my surroundings—my world that I left not loving."

Anita Calero

Anita Calero

and influences. In her homes, found items are stationed alongside pedigreed design pieces, insect specimens juxtaposed with books. The whole cacophony is then meticulously organized so that the assortment never veers into messy territory. "I dislike the fact that I'm labeled as a collector," Anita says. "A 'collection' sounds like you don't touch anything. I lived with my stuff—I sat on my chairs!" In *The New York Times*, esteemed critic Pilar Viladas once wrote that her apartment in New York's Chelsea neighborhood was "simple and unadorned, yet quite elegant—rather like Anita herself. Her domestic aesthetic embraces materials both rugged and fine, forms both imperfect and perfect, and objects both humble and luxurious."

"She nailed me in so few words," Anita says.

Though she lived in that apartment for 21 years—"it was my temple," she says—Anita sold it in 2013 along with her prized assortment of mid-century furniture, which included pieces from Jean Prouvé, Charlotte Perriand, Serge Mouille and George Nakashima, as well as Irving Penn photographs and other objects picked up over the years. But it was all part of the plan: Anita always knew she would retire in Colombia and had set a target to move back when she was 60 years old. Though she still travels to the US and Europe for shoots—"it feels good to still be a little part of the map in New York; it keeps me alive, motivated and inspired"—the moment had come to return to her home country's embrace.

After all, Anita's time abroad had come with its fair share of character-building hard knocks. She lost many friends to AIDS in the midst of the crisis in the '80s and '90s (including Maria's brother, Roberto), as well as two loved ones to cancer: one of her siblings and stylist Barbara Fierros, her partner after Maria, whom she was with for 13 years. But despite mourning the people who have left her side, she remains positive in the face of adversity—and thankful. "I'm lucky to be at this moment in my life," she says. In the end, the decision to dismantle her temple and relocate back to Cali was bittersweet. "I was emotional," she says, "but I was liberated, too."

In her headstrong early years, Anita was eager to escape Colombia so that she could forge her own path in the world. But now that her journey was beginning to come full circle, her impulse for a fresh start was about just that: going back to the start. "I missed my roots, my soil, my birds, my smells, my fruit, my surroundings—my world that I left not loving," she says. "If I had stayed in Colombia, I would've married a boyfriend I had at the time—I would've become a lady who lunches. But coming back was what I needed."

"I went to the school of Studio 54. It was hard to get into: You had to have the look, because if you didn't have the little outfit that brought the circus inside, you weren't welcome."

Anita now splits her time between Colombia and Barcelona, where her partner for the last eight years—Gemma Comas, an accomplished photographer who was formerly Anita's assistant—is based. Though Anita finds comfort in returning home, she welcomes the cosmopolitanism that globe-trotting offers her. "Colombia is nature, peace, family, roots and old friends," she says. "But Barcelona is culture, art, different foods and the old world. I like having those two things combined—I need it."

Though she's parted with much of the furniture she owned for 20 years—a necessity of moving into a smaller home on a different continent—some of it came with her to Colombia, such as a table she co-designed with Mira Nakashima. With a smattering of classic pieces and personal touches, it's an unfussy and livable space made special through Anita's artfully displayed flea market finds, preserved butterflies, artifacts and countless family photos.

Her new home is tucked in the forest and exudes a similar sensibility as her former apartment, despite being situated in a totally disparate context. The two-bedroom house—which she designed, just as her parents did her childhood home—is open and airy with high ceilings and a mix of tactile materials like local woods, brick and polished concrete floors punctuated with river pebbles. "It's very integrated with nature," she says.

Decks wrap around the perimeter as a transitional space between the enclosed rooms and the great outdoors, and wind blows through the doors and windows, permeating the house with the smell of fresh, wild air. "There are birds, butterflies, iguanas, every kind of animal coming inside," she says. "It feels very much like a treehouse." Her garden is filled with native species such as grasses, ferns and big-leaved botanicals, as well as a few orchids near the entrance. Last Christmas she even planted an olive tree to commemorate her beloved dog that passed away—her new dog, Lulow, now spends his days running rings around the house and garden.

While her hillside oasis is modestly sized, it's still expansive enough for Anita's extended family to come visit, just as they did for her birthday weekend last year. Anita is very close with her four living siblings, all of whom live in Cali except for a sister who resides in Medellín, a city 270 miles north. (Her brother's house is even conveniently next door.) Between her 10 nieces and nephews and their nine children, there's a constant cycle of baptisms, graduations and birthdays that she never had the chance to attend when living in New York. "There were many events that I missed—like my mother's 80th birthday and first communions—and now I'm kind of catching up with the next generation," she says.

This year, Anita is taking advantage of having extra time by regularly visiting her beach house on the Colombian coast and re-immersing herself in painting, her first medium. Indeed, youthful restlessness and zeal for being in a perpetual state of "doing" hasn't left Anita, and it likely never will. "I can't imagine just sitting in a chair, reading a book, with the beautiful view from my house," she says. "It's not me."

Left: Anita was celebrating her 63rd birthday on the day these photographs were taken. Here, she is holding up one of her favorite images from photographer Alfred Stieglitz's book of portraits of his wife, painter Georgia O'Keeffe. *Hold Still*, the memoir by acclaimed photographer Sally Mann, also rests in her lap. While Anita appreciates the convenience of digital photography, there are moments when she misses the simplicity and intimacy afforded by film.

PHOTOGRAPHS
PELLE CRÉPIN

STYLING
CAROLYNE RAPP

CASTING
ANJA GILDUM

Throwing

Shade

If home is wherever we lay our hats, then travel is an opportunity to change into a new one. Whether you need a wide brim to protect your eyes from the sun's glare or something to simply hide your sea-soaked hair, there's a hat for every occasion.

Previous page:
She wears a hat by
Henrik Vibskov and
top by Totême
This page: Hat by Co,
top by Norse Projects
and trousers by COS

She wears a hat
by Cheap Monday
and top by Studio
Nicholson

She wears a hat by
Lock & Co. Hatters and
top by Wood Wood

She wears a hat
by Norse Projects,
shirt dress by Hope
and dress by COS

She wears a
hat by Henrik
Vibskov and top
by LF Markey

She wears a hat
by Co and top by
Norse Projects

She wears a hat by
Weekday, shirt by
Filippa K and skirt
by Studio Nicholson

WORDS
ADRIENNE MATEI

NEITHER HERE NOR THERE

Modern travelers don't use guidebooks—instead, new tools help secure the meaningful experiences we crave. Yet when we embark on journeys with translator apps and spaghetti piles of charger cords, where is it that we really go?

It's rare to hear anyone say that they've traveled too much or that there's no place they'd like to go. As conversations about dream destinations unfold, it can seem that almost everyone nurtures a fantasy about some far-flung part of the world they've yet to see in person. Upon discovering someone in our midst who's been to that singular spot, we adopt the cross-legged enthusiasm of children at story time and beg them to tell us more. We listen attentively, take mental notes and vow to one day see it for ourselves. With our sense of wonder piqued, we then go home and Google obscure abbeys in Edinburgh or scroll through Instagram geotags in Mauritius, seeking even more insider information. This trading of knowledge can often turn traveling into an international game of capture the flag—our passports littered with stamps that mark off destinations from the constantly expanding itineraries in our minds.

To travel more often and further abroad has been one of the most consistent and widely shared human aspirations since the British began popularizing the Grand Tour of continental Europe in the 1600s. With its list of monuments and ruins to visit, these types of tourist trips became a hallmark of 17th-century bourgeois Western life. The premise behind why so many folks began packing their hatboxes and boarding steamships in the first place is the same that drives our wanderlust today: simply, that travel is thrilling.

"Instead of margaritas by the pool, many vacationers now seek opportunities to feel that they have learned and grown through their journeys."

When we approach an unknown land, our imaginations go Technicolor with anticipation. On arriving, the sensory overload of processing new surroundings is exhilarating: Days feel longer, details stand out sharply, we think more clearly and we become more energized. By shedding the routines to which we regularly adhere, we can discover sides of ourselves we didn't know we had.

"Tourists often return home feeling that they've captured a more true sense of self," says Dr. Andrew Alan Johnson, an assistant professor of anthropology at Princeton University. Based on his research (which is focused on the tourism and socio-political development of northern Thailand), Johnson suggests that the goal of obtaining a better understanding of foreign communities is at the very core of our desire to travel—just not in the terms typically defined by the global hospitality industry. This is because the way we travel and conceive of our priorities abroad is now beginning to change: Instead of margaritas by the pool at all-inclusive resorts, many modern vacationers seek opportunities for profound enrichment—to feel that they have learned and grown through their journeys. "Authenticity has become a signifier for value in Western tourism today," Johnson says.

"Authentic" has become the buzzword for the types of experiences many modern travelers seek. As a 2011 study by the United Nations World Tourism Organization revealed, "The postmodern consumer's search for experiences that are engaging, personable, memorable—and above all *authentic*—is especially strong in respect of tourism." Clusters of fanny pack–toting tourists checking sightseeing boxes by unquestioningly following their tour guide, looking to the left and right in synchronous obedience, are not as common as they were a decade ago.

Instead, today's travelers overwhelmingly judge the quality of their trips by the cultural and personal enlightenment they find. "Just as our parents' generation might have competed over the number of monuments seen, the quality of the cruise dinner buffet or the artistry of the luau performance, we now compete over the remoteness of the location and the 'genuine' response of the 'locals,'" Johnson says.

Yet paradoxes are at work within the complex concept of hunting down authenticity. "Some people don't actually want an authentic experience," Johnson says. He uses the example of organizing a trip to be "adopted" into a tribal group for a week's stay in the mountains of Laos: After working into the rhythms of life for a while, the tourist might feel like they're living like a true local. "But to be adopted—really adopted—in such a society means that you're a part of a kinship group. And you have obligations to your kin," he says. If they really had become part of tribal life, the "adopted" tourist would be required to divide their money among their new family and might feel offended at being told who they must marry. "Instead, they want to pick and choose," Johnson says. By stopping short of this truly local experience, travelers demonstrate the limitations of their interest in genuine authenticity.

"Just as our parents' generation might have competed over the number of monuments seen, we now compete over the remoteness of the location."

Because, if we're being honest, most travelers don't actually want to join a new community long-term—we just want a meaningful experience within the context of being a transient visitor and to return home feeling enriched by those encounters. But the question remains of how best to access these experiences. Cruises, resorts and guided excursions lack a certain coveted sense of freedom; it can be tough for us to spontaneously engage with locals and spur new friendships, hear about the area's up-and-coming musicians or be invited into someone's kitchen for a home-cooked meal. As a result, many modern travelers are eschewing the printed guidebooks that tourists in the '80s and '90s considered indispensable for trip planning. Instead, we're seeking tips of every stripe from blogs, social media accounts and travel apps to get past the periphery of a new place and catch a glimpse of its core.

The intersection of travel and technology is fertile ground for entrepreneurs seeking to help modern wanderers access the elusive, enriching experiences we crave. When she first visited China in 2007, Stephanie Lawrence developed an interest in exploring the country further, though she admits eventually returning home to San Francisco a little disappointed. "We had a very sterile, one-sided view of the country, and I felt that I hadn't had a chance to truly experience some of the gems—its incredible food, its warm and hospitable people, its vast history," she says.

"I saw glimpses, but we were mostly confined to buses, hotel rooms and the windowless hotel basement conference rooms where we ate with other tourists."

In 2009, Lawrence returned to Beijing for a six-month stay. During this time, she studied Mandarin and hoped to learn how to make *jiaozi*, one of China's traditional dumplings. She felt doing so would deepen her understanding of local food culture, but she couldn't find anyone to teach her. "That was my first light bulb," Lawrence says. This moment inspired her to cofound Traveling Spoon, an online service that connects travelers with local home cooks for informal culinary lessons. (Its slogan is *Travel off the Eaten Path*.) "It seemed strange that in a time when exceptional technology let me communicate with my family while I was living half a world away, there was no way to connect with the food and travel experiences I sought right where I already was."

Traveling Spoon now works with culinary hosts in 17 countries and counting—all of whom are vetted in-person by the company's team through a selection process that emphasizes their interest in sharing stories of their culture as much as their skills in the kitchen. "We have hosts outside of Kyoto, Japan, who will take you foraging for wild Japanese vegetables, and a mother in Kochi, India, who will teach you how to make *appams*, a delectable specialty from South India made with rice flour and coconut milk," Lawrence says.

"Our hope is that we can bring cultures together and connect people over the kitchen table by sharing recipes passed down to them through generations."

Lawrence's culinary company is one of a growing number of mobile or online communities offering travelers variations of sharing economy–based dining options that allow for direct interaction with locals in the communities they visit. For example, EatWith works with professional chefs in 30 countries who host pop-up dinners in their homes, and the US-oriented Feastly caters to travelers and locals alike. Both recall the sentiment expressed by American journalist and food writer Mark Kurlansky, who once said, "Food is a central activity of mankind and one of the single most significant trademarks of a culture." These technology companies seek to encourage strangers to connect over the nourishing ritual of a home-cooked meal, anywhere in the world.

But it's far from being just about foodies. Start-ups like Vayable allow locals who are passionate about a certain subject—say, architecture—to offer their services as independent tour guides, and Travelfy helps groups roving together stay organized and on top of mutual expenses. Online communities have also formed around sharing experiences—there's even an active "Stranded at an Airport, Tango Meet-up" Facebook group that exists for those who prefer to spend their layovers dancing.

Then there's the case of accommodation: The now-ubiquitous Airbnb provides an alternative to hotel chains (not to mention a chance to practice your Croatian with a Dalmatian family under their grapevined trellis), and infinite niche sites allow even further personalization. In 2014, an Airbnb survey found that 85 percent of their guests wanted to "live like locals," and that's exactly what these services can offer in contrast to a stale list of hotels in an outdated Lonely Planet guide. The majority of the housing options offered on these websites are company-vetted and peer-reviewed in an effort to keep users safe and the quality high. Because while a dash of the

unexpected can add interest to a trip, danger and disappointment are still thoroughly undesirable.

When the nature of how to even define "authenticity" is so fraught with complication, it seems wise to stay mindful of our own preconceived illusions of how we "should" experience new places in the first place; after all, enlightenment isn't always found in expected places. In *The Art of Travel*, Alain de Botton describes finding a purity of feeling in a location nobody would cite as a dream destination: a cafeteria on the side of a highway. Something about its isolation, its lack of pretense and the way it belonged solely to weary travelers pulling off the road to stretch their legs and eat inspired an introspective existential episode. "Its appeal made me think of certain other equally and unexpectedly poetic traveling places—airport terminals, harbors, train stations and motels..." he writes.

Alain de Botton was not the first writer to note this: When fed up with the monotony of daily life, poet Charles Baudelaire would "leave for the leaving's sake" and journey to a harbor or train station to watch the arrivals and departures. Poet T.S. Eliot hence referred to Baudelaire as the creator of the "*poésie des stations-service*" and the "*poésie des aéroports*"—the "poetry of service stations" and the "poetry of airports." These in-between spaces gain energy and character from their association with travel but remain untouched by its glamour—and they are all the more poignant for it.

But what is at the root of this philosophical search for authenticity? Two influential demographics in particular are shifting the travel paradigm.

First, there are millennials. As young adults emerge from universities into an insecure job market, many of the lucky ones are opting for an alternate route to further their growth through forays abroad. Travel apps and sites, which are often geared toward these budget-conscious travelers, promote rented rooms and home-cooked meals over big-name hotels and Michelin-starred restaurants. Recently, the World

Youth Student and Educational Travel Confederation polled more than 34,000 people from 137 countries to find that young travelers are simply less interested in the "traditional sun, sea and sand holidays" and instead prefer to immerse themselves in their destination's flow of life. On top of that, an additional 22 percent even aimed to pick up a new language while traveling. By virtue of treating travel as a life experience rather than a quick diversion from reality, younger travelers have championed the idea that mindful, immersive travel is the way forward.

At the other end of the spectrum, more mature and typically wealthier travelers are looking to diversify their experiences from the homogenous vacations they've already found at resorts. A study by luxury travel firm Virtuoso found that one of 2014's fastest-growing types of travel was in the luxury adventure sector: With a median age of 48, these are wayfarers who want active, fulfilling vacations that go beyond the norm—while still being prepared to pay for creature comforts. In this way, the pursuit of authenticity is a reflection of a growing urge to forge our own paths and fulfill our ideals, at any stage of life.

Most modern travelers seek experiences of personal significance and want to be enlightened as individuals. Yet many of us seem to consider documenting our journeys to be almost as important as making them. A 2014 survey by British travel company Sunshine revealed one of the top reasons respondents used technology while abroad was "to brag about my holiday." A Chase Card Services survey from the same year discovered that, despite having "a desire to unplug" while traveling, 97 percent of millennial respondents shared experiences via social media while vacationing, and 73 percent updated their feeds daily. The irony of consistently documenting our travel experiences on social media is that it removes us from the moment we are ostensibly enjoying.

"When a person is focused on their device, they aren't paying attention to the environment they're in," says Nancy Colier, a psychotherapist and author of the upcoming book *The Power of Off: The Mindful Way to Stay Sane in a Virtual World*. "Downtime is important to have. For example, long train rides are like wombs for creativity—just sitting in them and thinking without entertainment." In Colier's view, we benefit from consciously committing to being present where we are and using technology not out of idle habit, but only when necessary.

Social media and travel apps that provide information on the go have not only changed how we act while on vacation, but also how we prepare for trips. When planning our itineraries, many of us now look to Instagram feeds and travel blogs for inspiration. In fact, a 2015 PRSA Travel & Tourism poll found 84 percent of Facebook users say vacation images posted by their friends influence their travel decisions, and the ITB World Travel Trends Report 2014/2015 issued by ITB Berlin revealed 92 percent of social media users are influenced by travel blogs, with up to 72 percent willing to change their destination choice based on the opinions of friends and bloggers. "Discovering things once had to be organic—you would meet someone at a bar who would suggest you visit their friend who might know of a great place to stay," Colier says. While we used to seek these tips from our networks face-to-face, we've now removed the personal element of fact-finding in favor of having a veritable library of experiences to mine at our fingertips. "It's tricky," she says, "because although technology provides many interesting advantages, you also have to wonder if we're manufacturing authentic experiences."

And here's where the spiral begins: It's easy to be miffed when your favorite little bakery in Paris with its incredible *kouign-amann* is geotagged by an influential travel blogger and suddenly catapulted to fame when *The New York Times'* travel section picks up on it a week later. Closer to home, we see the same thing happen to our secret swimming holes, the elusive queue-less brunch spots and the best dive bars on the

"As technology makes it easier to be influenced by a web-wide consensus of what constitutes 'cool,' we now must work harder to find places truly off the beaten path."

outskirts of town. We have a tendency to feel protective of the places we love, and revealing those admirations only puts those special spots in the sightlines of travelers eager to appear "in the loop." By sharing our under-the-radar favorites, we unintentionally set them on their path to popularity. And as technology makes it easier to be influenced by a web-wide consensus of what constitutes "cool," we now must work harder than ever to find places truly off the beaten path.

In order to preserve their niche appeal, more vacation destinations are consciously attempting to stay under the radar. Susan and John Johnson, who run the low-key luxe Harmony Hotel in Nosara, Costa Rica, are intent on enriching rather than disrupting their surrounding small community. While they welcome guests and neighbors to their grounds, they actively discourage some of the free promotion and exposure other businesses would delight in—John has even asked certain high-profile individuals staying with them not to hashtag the hotel or the town in their Instagram or Twitter feeds. "Guests have told us, 'This is my new favorite hotel—I'm going to tell all my friends!'" Susan says. "And we've said, 'Just tell your best friend!'"

When a place becomes of keen interest to tourists, its local community is directly affected. Jennie Germann Molz, a professor of sociology at the College of the Holy Cross in Worcester, Massachusetts, agrees with the Johnsons' social media policy for that reason. She has written at length on the intersection of technology, travel and

togetherness, and adds that if tourists are conflicted about sharing a destination—and truly care about how their actions will impact the place—they should communicate with the local residents to figure out the most ethical approach to documentation. "I would ask travelers to consider who will benefit and who will suffer from them sharing a destination on social media," she says. "Would the traveler benefit more than the local community? Are they just doing it to enhance their own reputation and get some likes on Facebook or Instagram, or would the local community benefit from more publicity and a potential increase in tourist visits?" Because while it might be annoying to have your favorite local brewery inundated by culinary tourists thanks to a *Time Out* tip-off, having your entire community's way of life interrupted by stampedes of snap-happy visitors could be truly destabilizing.

Travel deepens our sense of connection to others and links us to a global community with whom to share and learn from. It enhances our ability to understand ourselves within a broader context and allows us to discover firsthand that which we could've only previously imagined. Modern travel technology can help us realize the types of adventures to which we aspire—everything from cooking with locals to dancing between boarding gates—but it can also distract us from our initial aspirations just as easily. Despite their power and usefulness, technologies are merely tools—how they influence our journeys is contingent only on us.

INTERVIEW
GEORGIA FRANCES KING

PHOTOGRAPHS
NEIL BEDFORD

STYLING
ALPHA VOMERO

Bring it on Home: Leon Bridges

From bussing tables at a Tex-Mex restaurant to performing at the White House in just under two years, musician Leon Bridges has no plans to part ways with his humble beginnings. Clad in Western-influenced threads and with a sound reminiscent of '60s icons Sam Cooke and Otis Redding, he and his band are poised to bring soul into the new century while staying true to their Texan hometown.

The hearsay is true: Leon Bridges really is one of the nicest guys in the industry. Born in Georgia to a Louisianan family, Leon lived in Atlanta and New Orleans until his parents moved him to Texas just before his third birthday. Twenty years later, a serendipitous meeting at a little honky-tonk in Fort Worth introduced him to friends and musicians Austin Jenkins and Josh Block, two Texan boys from the nearby towns of Weatherford and Waxahachie. The duo convinced Leon—who was dish-washing at the time and had never set foot in a professional studio—to come record with them, and the debut album they pieced together, *Coming Home*, was picked up by Columbia Records and eventually peaked at number six on the US charts.

Now 26, Leon recently played for President Obama at the White House and did a Lionel Richie tribute at the Grammy Awards with The Roots as his backing band. As a guy that could go any-where, he has decided to stay put and set up shop in the town of Fort Worth, where he, Austin and Josh remain the best of friends as well as bandmates.

When did you guys all first meet? — *Leon:* I used to play sets every Tuesday night at this place called the Magnolia Motor Lounge—I'd get off work bussing tables and would run over there and play two or three songs in between the bands' sets.

Austin: I was watching a friend's band play, and after the first set Leon asked to borrow my friend's guitar and got up on stage by himself and started performing. I still remember how I felt when I heard him break into the first song, which was "Coming Home"—it was completely life changing. It felt wonderful to hear someone singing like that with this vibe at a local bar on a Tuesday. When he finished playing, I forced him to talk to me near the bar...

Leon: ... and then it got weird! When I first saw him, I was like, "Man, there is a glow about this dude." I had never seen anybody with a cowboy hat wearing this kind of high-waisted Wranglers hanging around this little part of Fort Worth.

Austin: It was funny, because I realized that I had actually already met him a week earlier, but I had no idea that he played music then. We first bonded over—this is not a joke—pants. We were at

a bar and my girlfriend at the time went up to Leon and said, "You *have* to meet my boyfriend. He also wears those insanely ridiculous high-waisted Wrangler jeans à la [country music star] George Strait." We took a photo and talked, but we didn't talk about music. Then a week later, I see him play, and I remember calling Josh and saying, "Man, you're never going to believe what I just heard. You've got to check this guy out."

Leon: Austin said, "Those were some great songs. Y'know, it'd be great to record—live, straight to tape, and let's do it in the classic, old country, rhythm and blues style." He left, and the bartender was like, "… d'you know who that was?" and I said, "… no?" And he said, "That's Austin Jenkins from White Denim!" And I was like, "… who's White Denim?"

Austin and Josh, by that stage in your career you had both done pretty well with White Denim. When the three of you started recording together, did it feel like a mentor/mentee relationship?
— *Austin:* I'm not sure if we were *mentors* or anything…

Leon: That's how it felt to me though. I didn't have everything together, and I still don't have everything together! I just had a bunch of these songs on acoustic guitar—I didn't really know anything about the technical side of music, so it was good to have some people who have been around the block a few times to really steer me the right way.

Austin: It was kind of perfect timing on our end. Josh and I had been talking about putting a studio together and working with people for about a year prior to that. It was a really cool marriage of ideas, and it was equal footing in terms of excitement—everyone was really engaged from the start. We put a studio together in a day and recorded as many songs as we could in four days.

Josh: I don't think I had made music with somebody who had such a healthy lack of cynicism around other musicians as Leon did—he had such a great nature. So from our point of view, there was a lot for us to learn too. Musicians end up getting pretty strange heads after a certain number of years, so it was nice. The mentorship definitely went both ways.

"I love showing the world our perspective on soul. I could get on the mic and start screaming like a preacher, but we're not doing a James Brown or a Daptone thing—it's a Texan thing."

It sounds like the three of you filled in the things in each other's lives that had been missing before that. — *Leon:* Definitely.
Austin: Yeah, that makes a lot of sense. There's definitely a symbiosis of all those ideas there. Different people have different strengths and weaknesses… The best part about it is when you form a team, trust people and are genuinely excited about working together, everything else irons itself out.

Have you ever thought about what would have happened if someone that night had said, "You know what? Let's just stay in tonight and order a pizza?" — *Leon:* You know, I think it would've possibly happened, but it wouldn't have happened in the right way—we might've recorded in some modern studio instead. So it all was meant to be.
Josh: When we got in the studio together, we weren't thinking dollar signs: We were thinking, "This is a community."
Austin: That's what the whole recording process was about. We had no idea that it was going to turn into a record that Columbia would release! We were doing it because I believed in Leon's music, Josh believed in Leon's music and, most importantly, *Leon* believed in Leon's music. It was pretty wild.

Austin and Josh, you two have opened up your own full-time recording studio in Fort Worth called Niles City Sound. Is it fully operational now? — *Josh:* Rockin' and rollin'!

I've heard the public can go in and watch sessions live, and you can also record straight to broadcast, which was quite common in the '60s—people in that era used to listen to and experience music in a much more open, communal way. Did you consciously try to mirror that model when you were building your studio? — *Austin:* Yes, that was the initial idea behind it. Josh and I had talked about making the studio similar to a local Western thing called The Big D Jamboree, which was a '50s radio program that specialized in local talent and touring artists who would come through and want to be part of a radio show. They'd have live, straight-to-broadcast concerts so that people who couldn't be at the gig could be listening. That was the impetus for the studio, and we still try to keep that same ethos.

In opening Niles City Sound, you've invested a lot of time and energy into Fort Worth, which means you're probably going to be sticking around for a long time… You're proving that people can break the mold and make music careers outside of major cities. — *Austin:* That's the whole point—and I think that's the movement in a lot of places right now. You don't have to move to New York, London, LA or take your briefcase to Nashville to show off those ideas! You can create a little hub like this. We either really believe in that and love Fort Worth… or we're completely insane.
Leon: I wouldn't knock anybody who wants to move out of their hometown and make things happen, but I think it's more cool when you stay where you are. For me, I couldn't move out because, even if I had wanted to, I didn't have the money. So it was about staying in town, grinding and doing the open mic thing.

If the environment you're craving isn't where you are, instead of going out and seeking it elsewhere, create it. — *Austin:* I love that. Someone once told me that if you're not happy where you are, moving doesn't solve that. You can make something wherever you are. The best way to affect change is within the community you're in. It's such a nice way to reach people because it's folks you're going to be working with or seeing on a daily basis. It's nice to get to know those people and have that kind of kinship.

How would you describe Fort Worth? — *Austin:* There's a laid-back sense of independence in the city. It's always been a place where there's art and culture and music and cuisine, but it's also always been a place of ranching and farming communities where people make a living doing what they want to do and living on their own terms. It has a really nice blend of those kinds of properties.
Leon: For me, I love it because I get to come back, go to the same places and reminisce about them. It keeps me grounded.

Leon, you hadn't ever been outside of America before all this happened. After leaving Fort Worth and touring so much, how do you see home differently? — *Leon:* I definitely miss home. I go to all these different places and meet different people and am the star of the show, so I look forward to being back home where it's low-key and I don't have to be "Leon Bridges" anymore. When I'm home,

For a day in Forth Worth, Leon suggests starting the morning at Salsa Limón for its trademark breakfast tacos. "It's a local legendary spot," he says. Next, browse the city's eclectic museum scene: "We have great art galleries, a couple of historic stockyards and cowgirl- and cowboy-influenced museums," Austin says. Once you're creatively satisfied, grab drinks on the town at Magnolia Motor Lounge or Lola's Saloon. "You can walk in there any night and there's always some good music going on," Leon says. "Every now and then, I still get my guitar and sing a few songs."

"Even if The Roots wanted to be my band, I wouldn't do it. It's about more than loyalty: These guys are super badass players, good people and some of my best friends."

I don't do anything—I just sit on my couch and watch cartoons! It's always a joy on that last day of tour, knowing I'm coming back home and I get to roll down the street and see my 'migos.

Which other communities outside of the music world also mean a lot to you? — *Austin:* You're gonna be hard-pressed to find a Texas boy from around here that didn't do his due diligence in a church community! That was some of the first real music I sang and heard. It's a big part of the culture here, especially in the small towns. I feel like Leon and I bonded over that.
Leon: Living in the Bible Belt, the church community was the first time I felt like a part of something or had friends, so I've taken that with me—that's how I want everything to feel like when I'm on the road. It's great that the whole band knew each other from Fort Worth before this popped off.

Fuzzy tour vibes aside, the music industry can be pretty exclusive sometimes: Have you ever been made to feel like an outsider? —

Leon: What we're doing is different in a way, so you have some who love it and some who criticize it. Like, some people criticize the fact that I have a mostly white band, and I had somebody else recently ask, "Why are you wearing cowboy hats?" Well, we're from Texas, you know? It's just who we are! We're coming from Fort Worth, and we're doing soul music—I love showing the world our perspective on soul. I could easily get on the mic and start screaming like a preacher and get everybody riled up, but the way I do things is subtle. We're not going to do a James Brown thing or a Daptone thing—it's a Texan thing. Even if The Roots came to me and told me they wanted to be my band, I wouldn't do it. And it's about more than me just being loyal: These guys are super badass players, good people and some of my best friends.
Austin: It's really so top-down with Leon: His grace, vibe and humble spirit is completely apparent. As soon as you talk to Leon, you get it. The only criticism we've ever weathered has been purely speculative and has come from people who have never met us. The crew feels good. The sound guy feels good. The band feels good.

The management feels good… because *Leon* is good. It's a really simple principle, but it's transitive property—it gets passed along. *Leon:* It's cool—the criticizers will figure it out eventually. When I started this thing, I wanted to carry all my heritage. This sound is something my people started—but not only black people are entitled to soul music. Some people say that I'm alienated from my black audience, but I'm not putting a sign out telling my people not to come, you know? It is what it is. It just takes time, and I've already seen our audiences getting more diverse. This is the type of thing I wanted to pursue and this is what brings me joy to make, so this is what I'm going to continue to do. Our goal is to make good music.

Leon, I've heard whispers that you're still known to busk every now and then around town. — *Leon:* Yes, it's very true! I always look at it as never being too good to not still be playing on the street. I was in Dallas recently and there were these homeless guys busking—I recognized that people had worked out who I was, so I thought it'd be cool to sit down and play with them. At the end

of it, there was a hundred bucks in there! I love music: This is how I was before I got famous, and I'm still that person. When I'm on the subway in New York, I'll still pull out my guitar and start playing. I'm always touring, so it's just beautiful for me to get back to my old acoustic ways, because I don't get to do that much.

Well, now that you're back home before jetting off again, how are you going to spend one of your last quiet nights in Fort Worth? — *Austin:* I'll probably keep it pretty low-key—we don't have very much time at home, so it's nice to get that restful thing happening. *Leon:* I'm boring when it comes to time off! After this, I'll probably be on my couch with Netflix fired up. We're in the process of finishing some new songs that we're going to add to the set on this next tour. We want to make it bigger and better—we'll probably have some pyrotechnics here and there…

And a little bit of James Brown? — *Leon:* Yeah, I arrive on stage in a Hummer. Just kidding…

On pages 88 and 100 (top left), Leon wears a suit by Topshop, shirt by COS and his own shoes and socks. On pages 90 and 91, he wears a suit by Sandro, shirt by COS and his own shoes and socks. On pages 93 to 95, he wears his own clothes. On pages 96 and 102, he wears jeans by Levi's and his own singlet, shoes and socks. On pages 98 and 101, he wears a vintage shirt and trousers by Topshop. On page 99, he wears a vintage shirt and jeans by Levi's. On page 100 (bottom left), he wears a shirt by COS, trousers by Sandro and his own shoes and socks. Austin (below left, middle) and Josh (below left, right) wear their own clothes throughout.

GEORG JENSEN
DENMARK

MENU

1.
CRÈME BRULEE
FRENCH TOAST

2.
CRAB SALAD CLUB
SANDWICH

3.
SPICED DARK
CHOCOLATE DIPPED
CHERRIES
AND ORANGES

HOTEL
SP34

Lamp by Flos, pens,
stapler and tape
holder by HAY, clock
by Georg Jensen
and chair by Carl
Hansen & Søn

WORDS
TRAVIS ELBOROUGH

PHOTOGRAPHS
ANDERS SCHØNNEMANN

SET DESIGN
SOFIE BRÜNNER

The Room Service Menu

Instead of constructing tonight's dinner out of three-day-old fridge leftovers, let these recipes inspire you to indulge in life's little luxuries as seen in swanky hotels—heavy silverware and monogrammed napkins not included.

No one likes being taken for a tourist. Even if we're thousands of miles from our usual hangouts, we often want to believe we belong in a place, no matter how briefly we're visiting or how fanciful the idea. Fine hotels give us a sense that we matter in any location—the very purpose of their existence, after all, is to tend to our needs, make us feel at home and indulge our every childish whim as dotingly as any grandmother. Yet somewhat paradoxically, the secret to their success lies in treating guests unlike our ordinary personas and giving us an experience that we'd never usually bestow upon ourselves at home.

Take room service, for instance. First introduced in the 1930s by the Waldorf Astoria in New York, it embodies the concept of a hotel at its mightiest and most luxurious. Freed from dressing for dinner or having to encounter other guests, we can laze about and order nearly any delicacy we fancy and have it brought to our door. Our desires are heightened by our surroundings, which signal their difference from our mundane lives with every fixture and fitting. Where else but in a hotel do we encounter trouser presses or monogrammed towels, let alone individually wrapped miniature bars of soap and minibars laden with tiny

drinks? Would we ever painstakingly crease the ends of our toilet paper, or place a mint on our plump pillows? Inspired to indulge by add-ons such as these, we dial reception and order extravagantly. At an hour of the day when we might normally settle for a can of beer and a slice of leftover pizza, a bottle of champagne and a decadent sandwich suddenly seem like an excellent idea. Deep down, we know less is more and that the silver platters they're served upon are absurd, but through fleetingly relieving us of domestic concerns, hotels encourage us to occasionally embrace such luxuries with an easy conscience and a ready stomach.

RECIPE
DIANA YEN

FOOD STYLING
MIKKEL KARSTAD

SERVES 2 TO 4

CRÈME BRÛLÉE FRENCH TOAST

French toast is made even more special by giving it the flavors of crème brûlée. After being drenched in a rich custard, it's lightly coated in sugar before frying. The sugar browns, giving it a crispy, caramelized finish.

⅔ cup (130 grams) granulated
    sugar, divided
½ cup (120 milliliters) half-and-half
2 large eggs
½ teaspoon pure vanilla extract
½ teaspoon ground cinnamon
¼ teaspoon ground nutmeg
Salt
Four 1-inch-thick (2.5-centimeter)
    slices brioche or challah bread
2 tablespoons unsalted butter
Confectioners' sugar, for dusting
Sliced fresh strawberries, for serving
Maple syrup (optional)

In a medium bowl, whisk together ⅓ cup (65 grams) of the granulated sugar, the half-and-half, eggs, vanilla, cinnamon, nutmeg and a pinch of salt. Pour the custard into a baking dish large enough to hold the bread slices in a single layer. Place the bread slices in the custard and allow the first side to soak until half the custard has been absorbed, about 5 minutes. Flip the bread slices and soak until the remaining custard has been absorbed, about 5 minutes more.

Melt 1 tablespoon of the butter in a nonstick skillet over medium-high heat. Spread the remaining ⅓ cup (65 grams) granulated sugar onto a plate. Dip each bread slice into the sugar, coating both sides. Add 2 bread slices to the pan and cook until a deep brown crust forms, 2 to 3 minutes per side. (Reduce the heat as needed to prevent burning.) Wipe out the pan and repeat with the remaining tablespoon of butter and slices of bread. Sprinkle the toast with confectioners' sugar and garnish with fresh strawberries. Serve with maple syrup, if desired.

Tray and teapot by
Georg Jensen, napkin by
Georg Jensen Damask,
glass by Illums Bolighus,
large plate by Karin
Blach Nielsen, small
plate by Anette Friis
Brahe, cutlery by Gense
and cup, jug and round
tray by Kähler

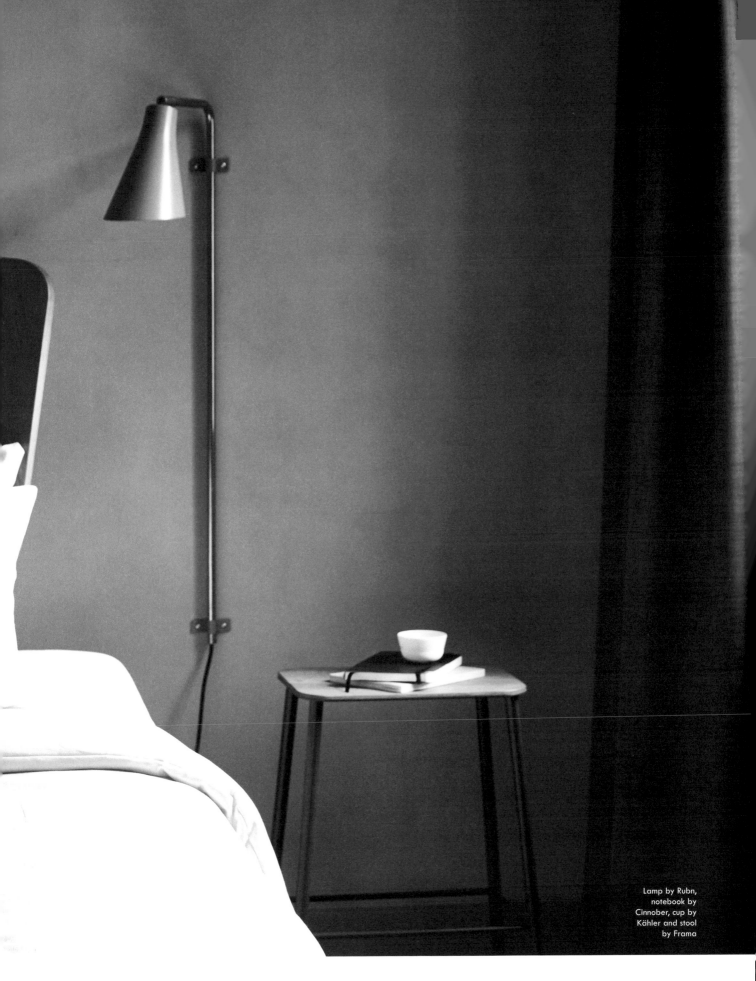

Lamp by Rubn,
notebook by
Cinnober, cup by
Kähler and stool
by Frama

Lamp by Rubn, cutlery
and carafe by Georg
Jensen, glasses by
Holmegaard, plate by
ferm LIVING and table
by Snedkergaarden

RECIPE
DIANA YEN

FOOD STYLING
MIKKEL KARSTAD

SERVES 2 TO 4

CRAB SALAD CLUB SANDWICH

A nod to the Northeastern lobster roll, this triple-decker sandwich is made with a smoky harissa mayonnaise to give it a spicy twist. It's a perfectly balanced combination of crunchy, creamy and refreshing.

FOR THE CRAB SALAD

½ cup (120 milliliters) mayonnaise

1½ tablespoons harissa paste

2 teaspoons fresh lemon juice

1 teaspoon dijon mustard

¼ cup (35 grams) finely chopped celery

2 teaspoons minced fresh chives

2 teaspoons minced fresh tarragon

8 ounces (225 grams) cooked crabmeat, picked over

FOR THE SANDWICHES

6 slices white bread, lightly toasted

1 avocado, halved, pitted, peeled and thinly sliced

8 thin slices vine-ripened tomatoes

6 slices cooked bacon, cut in half

Salt and freshly ground pepper

4 bibb lettuce leaves, halved

8 sandwich picks

TO MAKE THE CRAB SALAD

In a small bowl, mix together the mayonnaise and harissa. In a medium bowl, combine ¼ cup (60 milliliters) of the harissa mayonnaise with the lemon juice and mustard. Stir in the celery, chives and tarragon. Add the crabmeat and stir gently to combine without breaking the meat up.

TO MAKE EACH SANDWICH

Lay 3 of the bread slices on a clean work surface. Spread 1½ teaspoons of the remaining harissa mayonnaise on each slice. Set aside a slice for the top. Divide about half of the crab salad between the other 2 slices and top each with ¼ of the avocado slices, followed by 2 tomato slices. Season with salt and freshly ground pepper, then add 3 pieces of bacon and 2 lettuce leaves to each slice. Place one of the sandwich stacks on the other and top with the remaining slice of bread.

Pin the sandwich layers together by piercing them with picks in 4 quadrants, from the top slice of bread all the way through to the bottom slice. Repeat with the remaining ingredients to make the second sandwich. Using a serrated knife, cut each sandwich diagonally into 4 triangular pieces.

Left: Bathrobe by Rue
Verte, stool by Frama,
shaving brush by Acca
Kappa, shaving cream,
pre-shave oil and body
lotion by Barberians and
dish by Anne Black

RECIPE
DIANA YEN

FOOD STYLING
MIKKEL KARSTAD

SERVES 4 TO 6

DARK CHOCOLATE–DIPPED CHERRIES AND ORANGES

There's no better pairing than rich dark chocolate with the bright flavors of cherries and oranges, especially when they're sprinkled with a variety of garnishes to add texture and a punch of flavor.

6 ounces (170 grams) bittersweet dark chocolate (62 to 70 percent cacao), chopped

8 ounces (225 grams) bing or other sweet cherries, washed and dried

2 mandarin oranges, peeled and separated into sections

GARNISH OPTIONS

Chopped pistachios or other nuts

Shredded coconut

Flaky sea salt

Cacao nibs

Chopped hard pretzels

Chia seeds

Curry powder

Chopped freeze-dried strawberries

Granola

... or whatever else you fancy

Fill a medium saucepan with 1 inch (2.5 centimeters) of water and bring it to a simmer over medium-high heat. Line a baking sheet with parchment paper and have the fruit and garnishes at the ready.

Place the chocolate in a medium heatproof bowl and set the bowl over the pan of simmering water, making sure the water doesn't touch the bottom of the bowl. Stir the chocolate with a heatproof silicone spatula or wooden spoon until completely melted and smooth, 2 to 3 minutes. Remove the chocolate from the heat and use immediately.

Dip the fruit in the chocolate, allowing the excess to drip back into the bowl. (Save the remaining chocolate for another use.) Place the fruit on the parchment-lined baking sheet and sprinkle with desired garnishes. Some of our favorite combinations are shredded coconut with curry powder, chia seeds with granola and freeze-dried strawberries with pistachios.

Refrigerate for 15 minutes to allow the chocolate to set.

SPICY VARIATION

Stir in ½ teaspoon ground cinnamon and ¼ teaspoon cayenne pepper to the melted chocolate before dipping the fruit.

Trays by Skultuna,
forks by Gense and
champagne glass by
Rue Verte

Photographs shot on location
at Hotel SP34, which is part
of Brøchner Hotels,
in Copenhagen, Denmark.
Please note that while their
room service is delicious,
this menu was developed
exclusively for this story.

Tray by Stilleben, plate
by Kähler, cutlery by
Georg Jensen and
napkin by Georg Jensen
Damask

WORDS
CARA PARKS

PHOTOGRAPHS
ZOLTAN TOMBOR

STYLING
ALPHA VOMERO

A Day in the Life:
Justin Peck

With more than two dozen choreographies and legions of performances, Justin Peck is one of ballet's brightest prodigies. His dynamic works have earned him critical acclaim and precipitated his rapid rise to resident choreographer at New York City Ballet—just the second in the company's history. With his latest narrative ballet, "The Most Incredible Thing," Justin has attracted a fresh wave of followers to this classic art form.

Justin Peck is slumped in a chair along the mirrored wall of a practice room in the labyrinthine warren of offices, costume shops and studios that lies beneath New York City Ballet. He sits perfectly still watching a dancer move across the floor before suddenly standing and exploding into motion. "Try it like this, maybe," he says softly while leaping through the air, his hesitant voice at odds with the sureness of his motions. Then, just as quickly as he started, he quietly sits back down with a preternatural grace, once again wrapped in stillness.

With his arms propped up on the practice barre, Justin's leanly muscled dancer's frame gives him a slightly gangly appearance at rest. Paired with his tousled brown hair, he looks almost boyish sitting in the brightly lit rehearsal room. As he watches his dancers attempt the latest ballet he's choreographed—"The Most Incredible Thing," which premiered during the Ballet's winter season—his intense gaze reveals a determined focus that belies his youthful demeanor. Despite being only 28 years old, Justin has been a resident choreographer at New York City Ballet since 2014—only the second such person to occupy the role in the company's 68-year history. Like famed choreographer George Balanchine who, along with Lincoln Kirstein, founded the company in 1948, Justin's work has been credited with revitalizing the ballet world and bringing new audiences to the art form.

While many would see 13 as a rather tender age at which to begin a career, Justin is considered something of a late bloomer by ballet's exacting standards. After watching a performance by the American Ballet Theatre in his native San Diego, Justin was struck by the balance of athleticism and art in the dancers' performance and, despite having little experience with the form, embraced ballet with fervor. Though his parents exposed him to a broad range of the arts, they didn't foresee him becoming a dancer. "I had a wider array of outside influences and a more balanced childhood than so many professional dancers, who have to be focused in a very devoted and extreme way from such a young age," he says. "That probably helped me take the leap into becoming a choreographer."

At 15, Justin moved to New York to attend the School of American Ballet, the academy also founded by Balanchine and Kirstein that predates the company to which it is now attached. Today, the school is one of the most competitive in the country. "Most of my work was informed by my experiences as a teenager growing up at the School of American Ballet

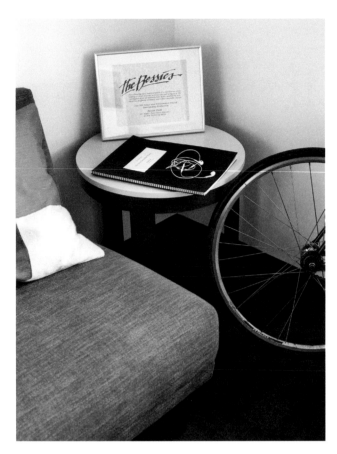

and seeing the repertoire at New York City Ballet," Justin says. As there's no single path to becoming a choreographer, it wasn't just his classes that guided his direction: The exposure to New York's dizzyingly dynamic cultural scene was its own type of education. His romance with Manhattan's metropolis endures to this day. "I've always felt like it's my home," he says. Justin's apartment is a 15-minute walk from the ballet's home at Lincoln Center on the Upper West Side, and he sees the city's frenetic movement with a choreographer's eye. "In one of my ballets ["The Year of the Rabbit"] there's a moment that was inspired by subway turnstiles: how they're designed and how people move through them in an efficient way," he says. "A lot of that can be explored through dance."

His choice of neighborhood is no coincidence. Given the amount of time Justin spends with the ballet company, a short commute is a prerequisite for a happy life. The demanding combination of being both the resident choreographer and a soloist dancer keeps him constantly occupied, as he's often choreographing one ballet and simultaneously performing as a dancer in another. He rises early most mornings, listening to the music he's working with and going over notes before leaving his apartment for the day. "It's a more meditative preparation than an active one," he says. "With every new piece of music I come across, there's a whole new world of thought. I'm lucky in that sense: A composer has to start from nothing and make something. I almost feel like I'm just facilitating this extension of music and sound."

After walking from his house to Lincoln Center, he attends the morning company class, which is a general warm-up session to help the dancers prepare their bodies for the day. He'll then juggle rehearsals for ballets in which he'll be dancing and those for which he's choreographing. At his busiest, Justin can spend six hours straight in rehearsals before performing in the evening, leaving little time for anything except a hurried meal before falling asleep.

But there are brief moments of respite: One season can be less demanding than another and breaks are sprinkled throughout, which allows Justin to cook, bike and attend performances in a more passive capacity. His girlfriend dances with the famed Miami City Ballet, so the pair split their time between the two cities, which provides each with a haven far from their core responsibilities. Even that remove is not a guaranteed break though, as Justin has choreographed for the Miami-based company as well. To maintain a sense of community while focusing intensely on his craft, he tries to include friends in his work, and he counts himself lucky that his family has joined him in relocating to New York and elsewhere on the East Coast. However, even that advantage can't solve every obstacle. "My dad and my stepmom actually live seven blocks away from me, and they often complain they don't get to see me enough," he says sheepishly. "But I always try to make time!"

Partly due to this punishing schedule, most people stop dancing once they are firmly established as choreographers. But Justin believes that continuing to dance is important for his development

Previous spread: These artworks were a gift from Marcel Dzama, who designed the costumes and scenery for "The Most Incredible Thing." Justin's apartment also contains creations by Shepard Fairey, Jessica Dessner, FAILE and his father, Samuel Peck. "Pretty much everything on my walls has personal significance," Justin says.

Left: Justin began dancing at age 13, which is rather late by ballet standards. Instead of seeing this as a disadvantage, he believes that his delayed start gave him a more balanced childhood. "I really came to it out of a self-found passion," he says.

Left: Justin decompresses after a long day by reading. Some of his favorite authors are Jonathan Franzen, David Foster Wallace and Haruki Murakami, and he also likes *The New Yorker* and *New York* magazine. He's currently reading Jack O'Brien's autobiography and *Wired to Create* by Scott Barry Kaufman.
Above: As both a soloist dancer and resident choreographer at New York City Ballet, Justin spends much of his time leaping and pacing across the floors of the company's many rehearsal rooms.

in both roles. "I feel like it keeps me grounded," he says. "I also get to interact with the dancers more, and I think that's an intangible thing that helps the quality of my work here. It's kind of a social art form, and everything's created in a communal way, more or less."

While joking with the other dancers in the practice room, this communal spirit is evident. Justin gives notes but also asks for feedback, inquiring how a certain step feels or looking for input into the emotional underpinnings of a courtship scene. The mood is one of collegial mutual appreciation, tinged by slight weariness. "I'm going to have a bloody mary at nine thirty and then I'm going back to bed until three," mutters one dancer as they discuss an upcoming day off, sparking general tittering and a broad smile from Justin.

"The Most Incredible Thing," which premiered in February, involves more than 50 dancers, including a gaggle of children from the company's school. The collaborative spirit extends beyond the dancers to two key contributors who were involved in the ballet's creation: Marcel Dzama, who designed the striking costumes and scenery, and Bryce Dessner, a composer and member of the band The National, who wrote the score.

Dessner's score was key to Justin's choreography; as is his custom, Justin spent many hours listening to the music to dream up his finished ballet. "A lot of it gets really nerdy—like, *mathematical*—deconstructing and getting inside the structure of a piece of music," Justin says. While he views his style as rather traditional ("inching forward kind of conservatively," as he puts it), Justin

enjoys working with contemporary composers. In the past he has collaborated with other pop-culture luminaries, including an ongoing partnership with singer-songwriter Sufjan Stevens. "I'm always eager to work with living composers," Justin says, "because the only way to maintain a sense of relevance with an art form is not to just create new choreography, but to create new bases for that choreography—new ideas and music specific to ballet and dance."

"The Most Incredible Thing" is based on a lesser-known Hans Christian Andersen fairy-tale. The fable tells the story of a king who promises half his kingdom and his daughter's hand in marriage to the person who can present his court with "the most incredible thing." A character named The Creator presents a clock that has a different display at each hour: Adam and Eve at two o'clock, the seasons at four, the deadly sins at seven, and so on until 12. The spectators declare it "the most incredible thing" until a villain called The Destroyer appears and, true to his name, destroys the clock. This repugnant act is even more unbelievable than the original creation, so the court is forced to acknowledge that this is "an even more incredible thing," and a marriage is reluctantly planned. However, before the ceremony can commence, the figures from the clock return to life, interrupting the proceedings. This rebirth transcends the destruction and is therefore proclaimed "the most, *most* incredible thing," and The Creator and The Princess are wed.

Narrative ballets such as "The Most Incredible Thing" may be popular with audiences, but they're also hard to pull off.

"The challenge," Justin says, "is finding a story that feels like it should be told through dance. Dance is sort of a flawed medium because you can't use words: It's a very specific parameter for storytelling." In Justin's interpretation of the fairy-tale, the clock's hours form 12 divertissements. Each time period is danced by small groups that grow larger with each hourly toll, culminating in the triumphant ending when dozens of dancers weave across the stage in a swirl of costumes including feathered outfits and rippling, abstract robes. With each timed segment, the dancers communicate different ideas—faith and chance and sin and the passing of time and the joy of children throwing sparkles into the air—in a heady production that builds to an emotional crescendo.

With the ballet's themes reflecting the enduring power of a seemingly transient creation, the story complements the limitations and possibilities that Justin sees in his discipline. "The story is about the lasting effect art can have on you, and how that's more important than the more materialistic aspect of art," Justin says. "It's very true to dance, because it's a fleeting, ephemeral art form, and once it's over, it's over—you'll never see that same thing again." What's left, Justin says, are the emotions and reactions that the dance provokes: the memory of the experience. Over the past few centuries, Andersen's creation, now reborn as a ballet, seems to whisper to this new incarnation. "Dead men cannot walk the earth," the Danish fabulist wrote. "That's true, but a work of art does not die. Its shape may be shattered, but the spirit of art cannot be broken."

Ballet regularly comes under fire for its lack of appeal and relevance to the current age. "In this country, ballet simply will not address the realities of the moment, and its reliance on flatulent nostalgia makes it hard to defend as a living art," once wrote Lewis Segal, the former *Los Angeles Times*' dance critic. Justin treads the line between looking back to his predecessors and drawing inspiration from his contemporaries. He is creating work that feels vibrant and unexpected and, in doing so, Justin has grabbed the attention of those outside the traditional ballet world. For example, he's choreographed a runway show for fashion darlings Opening Ceremony, and during intermissions for "The Most Incredible Thing," audiences could view a short film featuring comedian Amy Sedaris, which Dzama filmed for New York City Ballet's 2016 Art Series installation.

This is part of the reason words such as *prodigy* and *wunderkind* tend to follow Justin's name, but he refuses to see his achievements as the product of something other than putting in the many hours needed to excel. Instead, he credits the rigorous discipline instilled in a ballet dancer as an important factor in his success. "Balanchine used to say that there's no such thing as inspiration: There's just hard work and discipline. You get up and you work," Justin says. "I love that, because it takes the superstition out of art."

But push aside professional accomplishment and creative fulfillment, and surely there must be some way that Justin can be found wanting. "My apartment could probably be cleaner!" he admits. "Maybe there's a limit to the discipline in one's life in a given day."

Left: New York City Ballet performs its entire repertoire at the David H. Koch Theater at Lincoln Center. It was designed by architects Philip Johnson and John Burgee and opened in 1964 as a performance venue specifically for dance. The auditorium features five balconies and a large spherical chandelier.

PHOTOGRAPHS
ZOLTAN TOMBOR

STYLING
ALI & ANIKO

CASTING
SARAH BUNTER

On the Right Track

There's something transcendental about train travel: The speeding carriages not only take us from A to B, but also from era to era. This train—the Silver Arrow, used by former Hungarian communist leader János Kádár in the 1970s—now stands stationary at the Hungarian Railway Museum in Budapest. The ghosts of journeys past remind us that when time pauses as the world zips by outside, we can feel transported to a whole other age, not just another day.

Previous spread:
She wears a coat by
Samuji, top by GANT,
trousers by COS and
bag by USE Bag
Left: She wears a
shirt by Gucci and
trousers by Samuji
This page: She wears a
dress by Isabel Marant
and sunglasses by
MANIFESTO

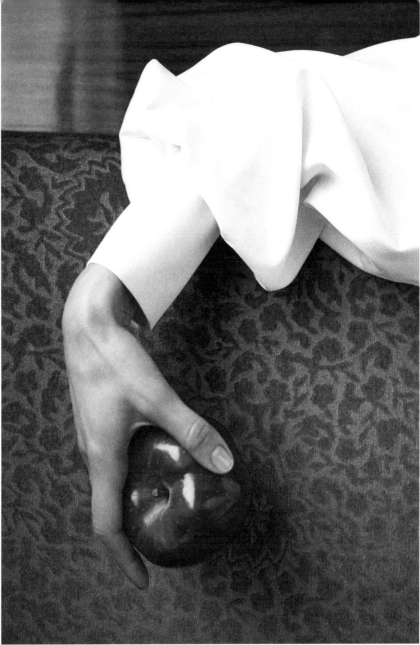

Left: She wears a
jacket by ÁERON
and top by COS
Above: She wears
a dress by ÁERON

She wears a jacket
by ÁERON and
jumpsuit by Hermès

This page: She wears
a top by Nanushka,
trousers by Samuji and
trainers by Converse
Right: She wears a top
by Paul Smith and
trousers by USE Unused

WORDS
RACHEL EVA LIM

PHOTOGRAPHS
NICOLE FRANZEN
KAORI ITO
KRISTOFER JOHNSSON
NOEL MANALILI
RAHEL WEISS

Profile Series
The Navigators

Cruising through Milan for Salone del Mobile, Paris for Fashion Week and Austin for SXSW: It's a working lifestyle many dream about. These worldly entrepreneurs may be based in London, Paris, Tokyo, Stockholm and New York, but they've also been lucky to traverse the outer edges of the globe. The founder of fashion boutique Creatures of Comfort, the product designer behind Note Design Studio and the editors in chief of POPEYE, The Happy Reader and Riposte all share their trip tips and favorite locations both at home and abroad.

PORTRAIT: KRISTOFER JOHNSSON; STILL LIFE: KAORI ITO

↓ Takahiro is pictured in his apartment where he lives with his family just outside Tokyo's busy city center.

↓ This tea set was designed by Sori Yanagi and can be found at Yanagi Shop, a small store on a quiet street in Tokyo.

TOKYO, JAPAN

Takahiro Kinoshita

As a world-wandering magazine editor, Takahiro Kinoshita relishes the moments he gets to spend in his home country by exploring Japan's lush natural landscape and logging some quality time with his family.

5 QUIET PLACES IN TOKYO

Yanagi Shop
It's very small, but I think it's very Tokyo: There's also a lab and workshop close by where the designer Sori Yanagi worked before he passed away.

Meikyoku Kissa Lion
You can escape the busyness and quietly drink a cup of coffee in this café in Shibuya.

Magnif
The neighborhood of Jinbōchō is famous for its secondhand bookstores. If you want to know more about the Japanese magazine subculture, I recommend this shop.

Genkido
Also located in Jinbōchō, this bookstore is particularly good for art and design books.

Tsuruhachi
This restaurant serves really delicious and traditional Edo-style sushi. You'll need to make a reservation and follow typical Japanese manners.

Though his frequent travels transport him to exotic locales, Takahiro Kinoshita keeps Japan close to his heart. The editor in chief of *POPEYE*, the much-loved men's fashion magazine, Takahiro was born and raised in the picturesque Shizuoka prefecture, south of Mount Fuji. He eventually moved north to Tokyo, where he currently lives in an apartment just outside of the city center with his wife and two young sons. "The first evening I have at home after a long trip is always spent with my family, listening to my sons' stories about what happened while I was away," he says. When it comes to escaping the hustle of Tokyo, Takahiro often likes to stay rooted in Japan instead of traveling far from home: For his next vacation, he hopes to make trips to Kōzu-shima and Aogashima, which are two isolated islands off the coast of Tokyo. While work keeps Takahiro busy, he also enjoys visiting Japan's many majestic national parks when he truly wants to relax. "Packing a tent, sleeping bag and food and hiking alone in the mountains—this time to myself is more luxurious than anything," he says, naming the ranges of Yatsugatake, Kamikōchi and Hotaka in the Northern Alps as his favorites. For people visiting Tokyo, Takahiro recommends classic areas such as Shinjuku, Aoyama and Ginza, but if they want to see the "real" Tokyo, he suggests heading to Mount Takao, which is a tranquil recreation area and nature reserve just an hour away from Shinjuku. "Sometimes you can lose a sense of the real Tokyo, but if you go to Mount Takao, you can see the average people who live in Tokyo in their true colors," he says. "You can also observe a view of Tokyo and Mount Fuji in the distance, which is another one of its appeals."

↓ Jade is pictured at Creatures of Comfort's office studio. They have retail outlets in New York and Los Angeles.

↓ Jade often heads to Russ & Daughters Cafe after a fashion show for the "best Jewish food in the world."

PHOTOGRAPHS: NICOLE FRANZEN

NEW YORK, NEW YORK

Jade Lai

A fashion designer's life is constantly in motion. Born in Asia and now the owner of bicoastal boutique Creatures of Comfort, Jade Lai has tied three locations together—Hong Kong, Los Angeles and New York—to form one concept of home.

5 PLACES TO EAT IN HONG KONG

Sushi Kuu
Really good, fresh sushi with stylish people. Get the house roll and the seared salmon sushi wrapped in lettuce.

Mak's Noodle
One of the oldest wonton noodle places in the city. They serve very small portions, so you can try a few things.

Lei Yue Mun
This is a fish market, so you get to pick your live fish and bring them to the restaurant of your choice—they'll then cook them up for you as you like.

Fook Lam Moon
I've been going there for dim sum since I was a kid. I think it's the best.

Spring Deer
This is an old-school Pekinese place. The shredded spicy beef pita pocket is delicious.

As fond of New York as Jade Lai is, there are times when she needs to escape. "I don't believe in staycations, because I can never really relax," she says while on an impromptu vacation in Tulum, Mexico. "I either end up being very lazy or feeling guilty that I'm not cleaning my house." Jade has always been on the move: After uprooting from her native Hong Kong to live in Los Angeles at age 15, she briefly attended boarding school in Seattle for a year before swapping back to Los Angeles' sunny shores. She then traded California for the speedy sidewalks of the Big Apple more than 15 years ago. Aside from preferring New York's faster pace, she also finds that its cultural diversity mirrors the internationalism of her Hong Kong home. "I like that there are lots of different cultural microcosms in close proximity to each other," she says. "Everything is very global, and everybody you meet brings their unique culture to the table." When she's not in New York or checking in at Creatures of Comfort's LA outpost, Jade goes to Paris thrice yearly, takes numerous production and sourcing trips and tries to visit one new country each year. As a former environmental design and architecture student, she gleans inspiration from the structures on her travels, such as the colonial architecture of Mexico City or Le Corbusier's Radiant City in Marseille, France. "I really like to look at things that have a bit of age," she says. "Places where you know the architecture has some warranty—that it has stood the test of time." The final regular trips Jade makes are her biannual ventures back to Hong Kong: Though she misses its dynamism and familiarity, she has no regrets about leaving her childhood home. "Unless you leave where you've grown up, you don't realize that the world is so big and there's so much more to see," she says.

Above: This gilt bronze statue of Diana, Roman goddess of the moon and the hunt, is located at the Metropolitan Museum of Art in New York, which is one of Jade's favorite museums. The statue was designed by American sculptor Augustus Saint-Gaudens and is the only female nude in his collection of work. The Met's version was constructed posthumously in 1928 from an original cement cast.

↓ Some of Danielle's recent trips include a month-long cycling escapade in Vietnam and a short jaunt to Lisbon, Portugal.

↓ Leila's Shop, a restaurant and grocery in Shoreditch, is one of Danielle's regular lunch spots.

PHOTOGRAPHS: RAHEL WEISS

LONDON, ENGLAND

Danielle Pender

Before moving to London, Danielle Pender's interactions with the city were restricted to the publications she devoured as a teen. Today, the editor in chief of Riposte magazine embraces the energizing nature of one of the world's creative hubs.

Growing up in the city of Newcastle in England's north, Danielle Pender never questioned whether she would eventually pack her bags and head south for London—it was only a matter of when. "I used to read magazines and blogs about what was going on and I just wanted to be a part of it," she says. Since anchoring herself in the British capital, Danielle has drawn on the vibrant energy of the community to inspire her working process. "The people who live here—the creative minds and the things they get up to—excite me the most," she says. These days she splits her time between her home in the northeast neighborhood of Walthamstow and her office in Shoreditch. The latter's central location houses a condensed cluster of the city's creatives, which makes it easy for Danielle to duck out for a meeting over a cup of tea. "London isn't as big or expensive as everyone makes out," she says. "It's essentially a collection of lots of villages, and you can live as cheaply or as extravagantly as you'd like." When she's craving a breather from city living, Danielle either hops across the Channel to Europe or ventures out into the English countryside: Two of her favorite vacation spots are Norfolk and the picturesque seaside town of Whitstable. "It's easy to get consumed by work and the daily grind, so it's good to remind yourself that there's more to life than your laptop and deadlines." Through founding *Riposte*, a magazine dedicated to creative women, Danielle now collaborates with a range of diverse contributors from across the globe. "You can create brilliant work with people wherever they are," she says. "That's one of my favorite parts of making a magazine: Being able to include voices, stories and visuals from people all over the world."

↓ Kristoffer was photographed at the Swedish Centre for Architecture and Design, where his studio was named Designer of the Year.

↓ Note Design Studio, Kristoffer's company, designed Fine Food, a restaurant in the Hammarby Sjöstad area.

STOCKHOLM, SWEDEN

Kristoffer Fagerström

Come rain or shine, this longtime Stockholm resident appreciates his city for all it has to offer, including its compact and casual nature, the up-and-coming restaurant scene and its proximity to Sweden's natural wonders.

Though Stockholm offers many wonderful virtues, Kristoffer Fagerström's connection with the Swedish capital is rooted in family. The partner and product designer at Note Design Studio was born in the city's Södermalm neighborhood. After spending his child-hood growing up with his two brothers in the southern municipality of Botkyrka, Kristoffer returned to Stockholm as an adult to start a family of his own. "I've traveled a lot, lived abroad and have really enjoyed my encounters with new cultures, people and experienc-es," he says, "but there's something special about Stockholm." From the shops, clubs and sporting arenas clustered around the city center to the nature reserves and beaches dotting Stockholm's archipelago, he loves the ease of navigating the entire city by bike—this geographic closeness has deepened his connection with the city and its community. "It's a well-functioning place and the people living here are tolerant and open-minded," he says. Kristoffer also takes full advantage of the region's rugged landscape: For exam-ple, when summer rolls around, he makes his way down the winding coast to Skåne Coun-ty, where both he and his partner have family. "That's our number one recharging spot," Kristoffer says. "Our little family spends at least four weeks there swimming, playing golf and doing nothing at all." When the long Nordic winter descends at the opposite end of the season, Kristoffer takes its arrival as an invitation to hit the slopes—though he's unfortunately had to scale back in recent years. "Last year I took my daughters to the north of Sweden on a snowboarding trip," he says. "But after a very humiliating session at the big jump park, I realized my extreme snowboarding days are behind me!"

Above: The Jeu de Paume museum, situated next to the Place de la Concorde in the city's expansive Tuileries Gardens, is one of Seb's favorite art galleries. The original building was constructed during Napoleon III's reign and initially housed tennis courts. Today, it's one of France's foremost contemporary art museums and hosts a series of rotating temporary exhibits.

↓ Seb makes quarterly two-week trips to London to work on each issue of *The Happy Reader* before it goes to print.

↓ La Cave de Belleville is a wine shop located in Seb's neighborhood. He's also a fan of the bar Le Relais de Belleville.

PHOTOGRAPHS: NOEL MANALILI

PARIS, FRANCE

Seb Emina

Culture-filled cobblestone streets, undiscovered pastry shops and getting wonderfully lost: The editor in chief of The Happy Reader and former Londoner revels in the adventure, romance and enduring mystique that comes with living in Paris.

5 BOOKS TO READ ABOUT TRAVEL

Granite Island — Dorothy Carrington
A book about Corsica from 1971 that's so beautifully written and comprehensively researched that it was made into a black cover Penguin Classic.

Venice — Jan Morris
I can't quite believe the city of Venice is real, and Jan Morris' masterpiece is an evocative approximation of the place and its history.

Letters from Hawaii — Mark Twain
Interesting, funny dispatches from four months Twain spent in Hawaii in 1866. I found my copy in a bookshop in Maui, and it still holds memories of that trip.

The North Water — Ian McGuire
I couldn't put it down. A dark, violent thriller set on a whaling mission to the Arctic.

The Rings of Saturn — W.G. Sebald
It's impossible to describe this book without sounding like someone trying to do justice to a disjointed but meaningful dream.

Since settling in Paris in 2013, Seb Emina has brushed off his French and adapted to the character of the City of Light. When he and his wife first arrived, they settled in the Fifth Arrondissement south of the Seine River, which is home to iconic Latin Quarter landmarks such as the Panthéon and the Sorbonne. "It's beautiful and traditional to the point of there being actual accordion players on street corners," Seb says. Now living in the Belleville district, which he loves for its creative vibe and multicultural atmosphere, he enjoys exploring the areas around the Belleville, Jourdain and Ménilmontant metro stations. "They're old working-class neighborhoods with vibrant Jewish, Chinese and North African communities," he says. "It's living proof that Paris is not just a museum city." After living most of his life in London, it took Seb some time to get accustomed to the relatively laid-back Parisian culture: With an emphasis placed on forging a healthy work/life balance, the French way of living was worlds away from Britain's hectic pace. "It's de rigueur for fashionable restaurants to be closed on weekends, and much of the city grinds to a halt in August," he explains. Seb has spent the past three years becoming acquainted with the city's geography without dimming the sense of wonder he associated with the metropolis before he called it home. While the number of mysterious alleyways and uncharted routes have gradually dwindled, he still relishes the moments that remind him of why he fell in love with Paris in the first place—such as the view of the Eiffel Tower from the top of his street and the myriad bakeries yet to be discovered. "There are times when I still feel like an outsider or a perpetual tourist—like I've only just scratched the surface of the city," Seb says. "But it also, somehow, feels like home."

IN CONVERSATION:

COLIN ELLARD AND PETER KAHN

INTERVIEW BY GEORGIA FRANCES KING

The advent of virtual reality is signaling a radical shift in how we approach travel: Soon we will be able to traipse around the world for the cost of a single virtual reality headset, journeying to far-flung destinations without ever leaving our couches. But it won't be all gimmicky antics and entertaining simulations: How will this new strand of technology permanently restructure the way we interact with our communities? And what repercussions will this have for how the next generation interprets the world around them? Cognitive neuroscientist Colin Ellard and psychologist Peter Kahn weigh in on the enduring value of physical travel and discuss how we'll be navigating the globe in the future.

Please introduce yourselves and what you study.

COLIN: I'm a cognitive neuroscientist. I'm interested in the relationships between brain states and behavior, and I have a special interest in how to apply what we know about behavior and neuroscience to issues like building better cities, which is a field called environmental psychology. In my laboratory, I do experiments that involve simulations in immersive virtual reality of different settings and scales—anything from the interior of a room up to urban-scale settings. The other side of my practice is finding ways to study people's psychological and physiological reactions to places "in the field." For example, we're taking people for walks through urban streetscapes and wiring them up with sensors to measure brain activity, eye movements and other variables to see how different kinds of settings influence how people feel.

PETER: I'm a professor at the University of Washington with dual appointments in the department of psychology and the school of environmental sciences. I also direct the Human Interaction with Nature and Technological Systems (HINTS) lab. I rarely use the term radical, but these two major trends—our changing interaction with both nature and technology—are radically restructuring human existence and have some major problems. First, the destruction of nature: It's happening very quickly, and it's happening to a kind of nature we depend upon physically and psychologically for our well-being. We're destroying the wellsprings of our very existence. The other trend is the exponential boom of technology: It's changing even faster than our linear minds think.

What are your reactions to the current climate of technological innovation? Is it helping or hindering us?

COLIN: There's this tremendous excitement in popular culture for the possibilities engendered by new technologies, like the [affordable virtual reality headset]

Oculus Rift in particular—people think it's going to have a completely mind-blowing impact on their experience of reality. But while people expect virtual reality (VR) to completely supplant physical reality, that doesn't really happen: It may happen for short periods of time in limited ways, but it's a somewhat confusing and disorienting hybrid reality that's hard to tolerate for more than a few minutes. For the people who have the impression that virtual reality is going to be an utter revolution in the way we interact with the world, I think there's some disappointment in the works.

PETER: Colin and I largely agree on this issue: There are benefits to new technologies, but almost every technology comes with costs. And we usually see the benefits and don't understand the costs until we jump forward with it. My lab's research on "technological nature" is not only looking at the benefits but also documenting the ways in which technology comes up short. Both my and Colin's research programs are trying to look at the positives and the negatives: We don't want to be naysayers about technology, but if you're going to ask the crucial question, "How do we flourish as human beings?" you need to pay attention to the costs.

How do you see VR tying into the future of travel?
COLIN: Especially with the advent of relatively cheap VR, there will be much more of an effort to use that technology for marketing travel and giving people curiosity about places. Having a small—but pale—taste of what being in a different place would be like might increase the likelihood of someone wanting to actually go there. But when I start to think about the negatives, there are all kinds of risks. First of all, somebody may feel that a VR experience of a place is an adequate substitute for being there. If they feel that the relatively superficial experience they've had is just as good as the real thing, then why bother getting off the couch? There are many negative repercussions and dangers with this kind of thinking. I've had these kinds of experiences with my children, and I've found a really alarming and stark contrast compared to my own experiences. For example, I took my children to see some moon rocks. I remember when I saw these things for the first time at a fairly young age, I was completely staggered by the fact that here were actual artifacts that had come from a different part of the solar system. But my children were just phlegmatic about the whole experience because it wasn't as good as looking at a simulated,

augmented version of a trip to the moon. What frightened me was that they didn't seem to have any kind of reverence for the authenticity of experience I remember having when I was a kid. It was almost as if that didn't matter anymore. That's the same kind of fear I have with virtual travel: We're finding even more ways to discount the value of authentic experience. If we can endlessly reproduce some kind of experience, then where is the value in having the actual experience? It's gone. It's tremendously important to go to another place in real time to experience cultural differences and not through some technological artifice. Otherwise, you don't really understand that you have a culture yourself.

Peter, what are your feelings about how VR is going to impact the future of travel?
PETER: I think of VR as something that is completely simulated—and that's problematic. The one thing that is wholly missing is an actual other person: This is the clearest way to articulate where the limitation lies. If you're traveling to a real location then you're likely meeting people and having authentic relationships, which is one of the marvelous qualities of being a human being—there's mystery in every interaction we have with one another. When you take that away with VR and engage with people as simulated computational models, my position, philosophically, is that none of that relationship is actually there anymore: There's no consciousness, there's no being, there's no presence in any genuine way. Going back to the issue that's overriding both my and Colin's research, I don't think we can flourish as individuals if we're not trying to deepen our experience of human-to-human interaction (as well as human-to-geography or human-to-nature interaction). And that's one of the large drawbacks of any sort of technologically mediated travel. I don't believe that it can substitute for the actual travel experience.

What are the long-term consequences of these kinds of technologies becoming commonplace?
PETER: As we allow these substitutions to happen and see the benefits, the big problem I see is that we start thinking that the impoverished experience is the normal experience; we're shifting the baseline of what's normal, but we don't even know it. Just like Colin's point with his kids, it's affecting an entire generation that has come along and constructed new baselines of what the new normal is—but they don't even realize that's

> "There are two questions we need to ask ourselves: Are there technologies we don't want to bring into our lives? And are there ways we can develop technologies to allow us to flourish instead of inhibiting us?"

the watered-down version because they've never known any different. If you put an elephant in a zoo and they have offspring, the babies may grow up to live long lives, but they are not flourishing as elephants based on their genetic makeup. As we increasingly engage in technological interactions—including technological travel—I'm worried that people will think we're doing just fine when, in fact, we're not doing as well as we could be if we were engaging in actual interaction.

In the future, we might be able to engineer the exact virtual travel experience we want to have instead of being exposed to the unknown—which is often the time when we learn the most. It seems to defy one of the main reasons many people travel in the first place. What will we lose when we gain more control over our experiences?

COLIN: I definitely agree with that. The kind of curated travel experience you're describing—where people prescribe all the experiences they expect to have before they leave their homes—just sounds absolutely dreadful to me. When I think of my own travel, the best experiences I've ever had have always been the serendipitous ones. If you go looking for specific stuff, then you're almost invariably disappointed. But if you just immerse yourself in a new setting and let what comes come, then those are the experiences you'll be telling your friends about when you get home, not the itinerary you laid out three weeks in advance. I can imagine that traveling using VR will inevitably be very prescriptive like that.

PETER: Serendipity is an interesting point to bring up, because if someone wanted to take the pro-technology position they could say, "Okay, tell me what you want

to happen serendipitously, and we can program that into the system." If what you want is a certain randomness, they can account for that. So the notion of serendipity goes beyond the behavioral fluctuation of randomness to something deeper: Georgia's point about the authenticity of interaction. The notion of authenticity operates at a phenomenological level that's tied to human consciousness and awareness. It's hard to articulate these ideas (and certainly harder to measure them from a scientific perspective), but here's what lies at the heart of the debate right now: Can all of human life be computationally modeled and represented, or is there something deeper to the human existence that goes beyond the computational system?

COLIN: Peter, what you're saying is really, really interesting. So, it would be possible for a programmer to produce a virtual travel experience that has every possible simulation of serendipity as a real travel experience? It sounds like the linchpin is the fact that we *know* one experience is simulated and we *know* that one is real, even if the simulation is perfect and the technologist can simulate all of the contingencies, the unexpectedness, the randomness. That knowledge ultimately seems to make a big difference to the experience's authenticity.

PETER: Yes, basically the technologist says, "Tell me what behavior you want and, in time, we can get it." At the core though, there's something deeper than the behavioral manifestation of the experience at play, and that's why I keep coming back to notions of authenticity through our actual, real experiences: genuineness, consciousness, awareness and a sense of presence that we engage in when interacting with one another.

"It's tremendously important to go to another place in real time to experience cultural differences and not through some technological artifice. Otherwise, you don't really understand that you have a culture yourself."

Surely there's a positive side to this: Could it be better for people who don't have the socio-economic means to actually travel to have these virtual experiences that they know aren't real, rather than having no access to these experiences at all?

PETER: Based on my work on technological nature, if you can't have actual nature, then the technologically mediated experience of nature can give you *some* of the same psychological benefits as actual nature—but it doesn't give you *all* of the benefits. Part of nature's tremendous force in our lives—before we had so much control over it—is that we have to encounter it and work with it. That's powerful and beautiful. And actual, *real* travel taps into that.

COLIN: I would say that's true. I hate to be boring and agree with Peter so much, but I do! Something is better than nothing. One can think of all kinds of good reasons for offering virtual travel to people who can't afford to go on an exotic trip. But there are more examples too: Some years ago I had a conversation with a co-worker whose son is severely physically challenged, and she said, "I would love to think that he could put on one of these devices and take a jaunt to a rainforest—something he'll never be able to do in his actual life." There are other reasons as well, such as the places that would be fabulous to visit, but if lots and lots of people went there, they would wreck them. For example, if everybody who wanted to go to the Antarctic went there, it would have a huge environmental impact.

PETER: What I'm worried about though is that while we're well aware of the benefits, we're not aware of the drawbacks. We can paint the picture of how virtual travel or mediated travel is so wonderful, but I worry about the consumer culture around travel. *National Geographic* and webcams and TV are adding more and more to the information overload... which is tremendous in some ways, because our minds are increasingly able to consume smaller and smaller fragments of information. But, usually, people want something that they can digest in five minutes or five seconds.

How is that going to impact technological travel?

PETER: What is likely to happen is that many people are going to travel for 10 minutes or five minutes or 30 seconds. Many of the forms of serendipity that Colin and you were talking about earlier are uncomfortable in the beginning—a fear or wariness because you don't know what's about to happen. There's a part of our psyche that wants to limit that in our lives, but when you create a very focused itinerary and take control, you're eliminating much of the uneasiness of travel. And if you do that using a technological version of travel, that limits it even further. If at any point the technology starts making us uncomfortable, we will just turn it off or flip it to another channel. Out of the entire depth and range and beauty and mystery and horribleness of travel, we'll increasingly constrain that to a "nice" travel, and that's impoverishing the depths of human existence.

In what ways can you see technology being used positively in order for us to become more in touch with ourselves or our communities?

COLIN: One of the things that seems to be happening at the moment is this proliferation of apps whose intention is to give people ways of self-monitoring. Think of everything from fitness watches to apps that allow people to monitor their physiological state and stress levels throughout the day. You could talk about these being positive contributions of technology.

PETER: When you asked the question about some good uses, it often focuses us on individual applications of technology, and I think it can distort the larger picture when we think in that way. There can be some good in any single application we use, but we're not living with just a single app that we're trying to evaluate: There are millions of apps, and many of us have multiple devices working at one time. There are many benefits, but Colin and I are looking at the proliferation of this within us as a species. For every technology, there is a downside. Think about electric lighting: I love electric lights because they let me stay up late at night and read and converse with people, but electric lights blind me to the night sky. When a whole city has electric lights and I go out and look at the night sky, there *is* no night sky—there's just light pollution. So we need to talk about the individual use of a technology's effect on the larger system. Some kids—*millions* of kids—have never seen the stars because they've grown up in a polluted city. And that's really sad. But if you ask a child who's never seen the night sky if they feel sad, they say, "No, I don't feel sad... What's the night sky?" There are kids who don't believe that shooting stars exist—they think they're fictional because they've never seen one. We have now shifted the baseline to think that electric lights are a great technology, and we're never going back. We're adapting, but I don't think we're thriving.

I want to bring up Peter's elephant example from earlier on: Will the elephant's chemistry eventually change— physiologically, biologically, psychologically—and will humans therefore also start to adapt to this new technological environment? How will our increased dependence on these technologies change us over time?

COLIN: I think we're already seeing quite substantial mental changes, and the simple answer to the question of physical changes is the more time we spend sitting on the couch looking at screens, the less time we're actually physically interacting with the world. In terms of the crises in health-related occurrences such as obesity and the development of diabetes, I'm sure there are connections in terms of our overuse of technology and the fact we're becoming more and more sedentary.

PETER: Some people would say, "Don't worry about anything. We're an adaptive species, and that's how we got to be where we are. We'll adapt and we'll be fine." I think we're an adaptive species and we have evolved, but just because we adapt doesn't mean we'll do fine— it doesn't mean we're *doing* fine. If you look at the state of the world, there's a tremendous amount of disease right now: In the United States, at least one out of every 10 people takes antidepressants, and asthma is at a 7 percent rate. We're not doing that well, but we somehow think that's normal. And I don't think it is.

What kind of conversation should we be having in the meantime then?

PETER: What we need to bring forward—and I think we've been doing that in this conversation—is the richness and depth of what human life is about. We have been speaking about some of the benefits of technology, but that's not what thoughtful people need to spend a lot of time on: What we need to articulate is what we are *not* seeing as we move forward with these technologies. Then we have two questions we need to ask ourselves: Are there technologies we don't want to bring into our lives? And are there ways we can develop these technologies to allow us to flourish instead of inhibiting us?

Colin, some of your research has focused on GPS systems and wayfinding. What kind of impact are these programs having on travel?

COLIN: One of the things I've talked about is the influence of wayfinding technology on our understanding of where we actually are on the planet. As we become increasingly subservient to the blue dot on our phones, we eventually begin to lose touch with the meanings of even very simple geographic terms. When we replace the things we used to do by our native wit with technology, we lose a real understanding of where we are. When we lose an understanding of the meaning of scale and geographic distance, we lose the feeling of being connected to different places.

How far do we need to travel and for how long do we need to be disconnected in order to feel the benefits?

PETER: My daughter was recently trekking in Nepal, and she said that there's now Wi-Fi in all the small villages. She chose not to take her phone with her on these big mountain climbs, but everyone else was

"For the people who have the impression that virtual reality is going to be an utter revolution in the way we interact with the world, I think there's some disappointment in the works."

texting and blogging the whole way through. Traveling used to entail getting away from that endless stream of communication: It's this beautiful, profound pattern of moving away from settlement and returning, such as when we used to hunt and forage. Going out and returning is deep in our evolutionary history. In *Paradise Lost*, John Milton says, "Solitude sometimes is the best society, and short retirement urges sweet return." Now we go out and travel, but we still stay connected—we don't get to experience that pattern of "coming back" fully, because we never truly departed.

Colin, you've done a lot of research on the built environment. How have you seen cities try to encourage people to take vacations within their own boundaries instead of having to travel for that kind of experience?

COLIN: One of the most heartening things that the last couple of decades of research has shown over and over again is the powerful impact of exposure to nature in cities. I think that most decision makers are well aware that, in many places, there is a real appreciation for the importance of landscape architecture and the idea that there ought to be accessible green space for everyone, even if that's nothing more than a couple of park benches and an urban parkette. There's also been some discussion and interest in providing people with technology-free bubbles: locations in the city where your cell phone signal is blocked. If you can will yourself to go there, it's an aid that will help you disconnect with technology and reconnect with things that are more important to you than that.

Peter, any closing remarks?

PETER: I'd like to synthesize what I've been hearing: I propose that we travel for three reasons. One is we travel for cultural purposes—for amazing cities, music and art—to enrich our lives. The second is traveling for nature—people spend a lot of money and effort to get to beautiful places in the world. And the third one that we've been circling around is tied to the depth of our awareness and seeing our surroundings in a new way—and that's hard to replicate in a city we are so familiar with. I think that every day we should try to wake up and see our world with fresh eyes. But there's something about travel that forces us into this state automatically without having to work at it. Every time we leave what we know, we leave safety behind. In terms of technology, when we try to control too much of that experience and take the unknown out of travel, we're limiting this third dimension of what travel provides us, which is movement into the unknown. Through the unknown, we see more clearly, more deeply and then we become more fully ourselves.

COLIN ELLARD IS THE AUTHOR OF *PLACES OF THE HEART: THE PSYCHOGEOGRAPHY OF EVERYDAY LIFE* (BELLEVUE PRESS) AND *YOU ARE HERE* (DOUBLEDAY).

PETER KAHN IS THE AUTHOR OF *THE HUMAN RELATIONSHIP WITH NATURE: DEVELOPMENT AND CULTURE* (MIT PRESS), *TECHNOLOGICAL NATURE: ADAPTATION AND THE FUTURE OF HUMAN LIFE* (MIT PRESS) AND MORE.

PHOTOGRAPHS
AARON TILLEY

SET DESIGN
KYLE BEAN

Sincerely

Yours

The ease of modern communication conceals the distance between us, but keeping in touch long-distance hasn't always been as easy as simply hitting "send." Even though we're separated by seas, resorting to old-fashioned methods still gets our messages across—literally.

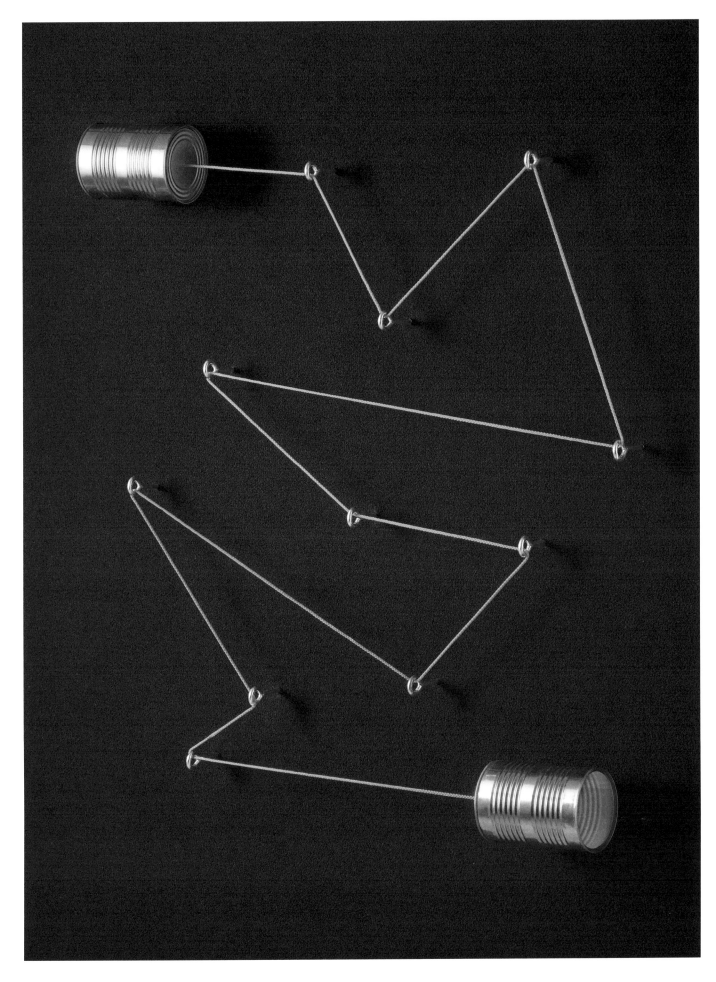

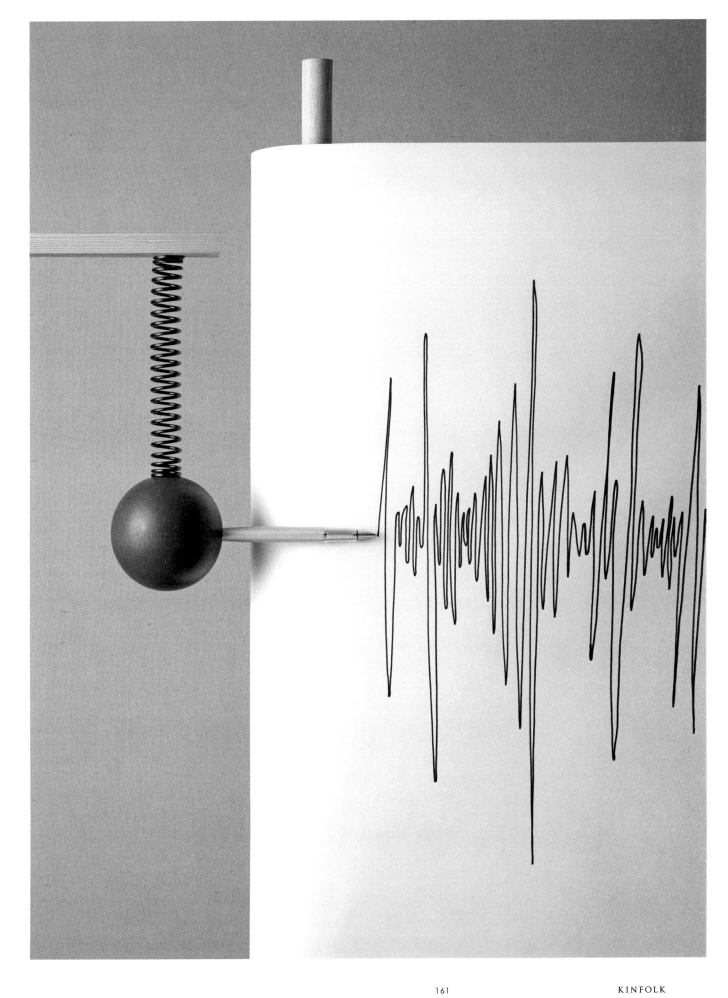

WORDS
ALICE CAVANAGH

PHOTOGRAPHS
ANDERS SCHØNNEMANN

Behind the Scenes:
Hotel Fontevraud

From keeping the hedges manicured to placing a tiny chocolate on our pillows, hotel staff silently tend to our every whim, so we rarely get to ask about theirs. We chat with the folks at the Hotel Fontevraud about working within the stunningly refurbished walls of one of France's most beautiful abbeys.

Among the countless luxury hotels dotting France's Loire Valley, Hotel Fontevraud, once a great monastic abbey with strong ties to the French royal family, stands apart from the rest. Recently revived and free from over-the-top tourist trappings, it has more regal prestige than most of the other Disneyland-esque châteaus in the countryside put together. From environmental considerations to soundproofing the great, cavernous communal areas, every aspect of the spacious and modern contemporary redesign has been treated with thoughtful consideration. While the hotel's interior is a tribute to modern architecture, the foundations date back to the 12th century, and the space has been furnished and decorated throughout with the kind of restraint that befits the pure and simple lifestyle of its earliest inhabitants: nuns and monks of the Benedictine order.

Founded in 1101 by preacher Robert d'Arbrissel (a trailblazer of sorts who made the controversial decision at the time to put a woman in charge), the Royal Fontevraud Abbey became a place where well-to-do women came for their education. Those who joined the order were required to take a vow of silence, which made for a pious and challenging life. However, it was also a sanctuary from the turbulent outside world, and—for many young noble-women—an escape from an undesirable marriage to suitors three times their age.

Following the French Revolution in the late 18th century, Napoleon seized the Abbey and converted it into a high-security prison. Murderers, thieves and political prisoners were held captive within its ironically picturesque confines. It became infamous for its harsh and overcrowded conditions, which were considered to be some of the worst in the country: In the mid-1800s, the life expectancy for an inmate was just eight months. Despite its significance as an important holy site, the Abbey remained a prison until 1963. After extensive restorations, it opened its doors to the public again in 1975 and began its third life as a community center for the neighboring population.

Today the Hotel Fontevraud—which was redesigned in 2014—is just one part of the larger site the local community supports: Along with artist residencies, contemporary art exhibitions, cultural events and tours through the remaining historical buildings of the Abbey, the vast grounds also boast a restaurant, a bar and easy access to the food, wine and sights of the Loire. It has been deemed a Cité idéale—one of France's very first "cultural resorts" that embraces living alongside the past.

TOUR GUIDE — Zoé Wozniak

What is your personal history with the Abbey? — I've worked here for a bit more than seven years. I grew up 20 kilometers (12.5 miles) from here, so the Abbey has always been part of my life: We used to come every so often to buy gifts, see concerts and have meals with family and friends. At first, I didn't realize that the history was so important: So many people lived here, suffered here, died here. I think some of the local population wants to forget that part of history: Even though they walk by the Abbey every day to go to the bakery, they never enter the site. But now I'm starting to understand the importance of it.

What is your favorite thing to tell visitors? — I like the medieval part of its history. The doors were shut for centuries, enclosing many people inside who couldn't get out, such as nuns and prisoners. Now we are trying to open the doors and get everyone inside.

TOWN RESIDENT — Christine Trouillas

What is your connection with this area? — I'm 71 and arrived here when I was six months old. After the war, my father worked for the Ministry of Justice and came to the prison to work. We were nine children and lived just outside the prison in a small house close to the church. I met my husband, Hubert, here—his father was a warden living in the village. We were married when we were 20 years old.

What was it like growing up in that environment? — When I was young, I didn't realize we were living in a prison. We didn't pay much attention because we were used to it—some of the prisoners were in the offices and gardens and weren't dressed like prisoners. But we knew that Fontevraud was an important historic place because there were always people visiting. Now, with the restorations, I am proud to be part of that history.

"I'm like a conductor: Without musicians, I would be useless! My role is to help everyone play their score perfectly in a collective creation and to provide enthusiasm and emotion for the audience."

GENERAL MANAGER — DAVID MARTIN

CURATOR — Emmanuel Morin

What's your favorite thing about your role? — When you walk
into a museum, you expect to see art on the walls, but the public
doesn't come to the Abbey for the art: They come to learn about
the history and heritage of the buildings. So when they're con-
fronted with great works of art—especially the large installations
we have on display here—it's an unexpected surprise. That's quite
a beautiful moment.

PUBLIC RELATIONS OFFICER — Olivier Châble

What do you like most about working at the Abbey? — I love to
learn languages—I speak French, Spanish, Italian, English, and I'm
learning German—and I really care about heritage. So the Royal
Abbey of Fontevraud is the perfect match for me. The most inspiring part is probably the team: There's a very strong link between
this place and us. We're a part of something that began 900 years
ago, and we're giving it a future.

> "It's my table for lovers: You are side by side and you can share the same view. Sometimes you remember very simple moments in your life, and this could be one of them."

INTERIOR ARCHITECT — PATRICK JOUIN

INTERIOR ARCHITECT AND FURNITURE DESIGNER — Patrick Jouin of Agence Jouin Manku

What was it like to work on this project? — My business partner Sanjit Manku and I were so thankful to be able to touch something like this: It's 12th century, so it's already beautiful. We're very lucky to have these buildings from the past in Europe, and we're often working on finding the tension between the past and present in our projects. The Abbey was a peaceful place, so we didn't have to do that much. Peace, I think, is the ultimate luxury.

What were your goals in redesigning the Fontevraud Abbey's interior? — I wanted to respect the past and to play with materials like wood, steel, fabric and leather: Natural materials connect you with a space, as they're not trying to pretend to be something they aren't.

As this is a heritage-listed site, there must have been huge restrictions to what you could do. What were the greatest practical challenges? — Keeping out the cold and soundproofing the space were the biggest challenges: A chapel is for people to sing or pray in, not to drink or chatter in, so we

had a lot of echoing! But the constraints encouraged problem-solving—we couldn't take anything out, so we had to mix aesthetic with function. In the end, we put up a big wall of fabric to help with the sound and provide heat insulation. We also introduced a heater under the flooring using an old Roman technique with hot water. We had to work with an architect who looks after historical monuments—he's the only person who could touch it.

How did you approach designing the rooms? — Our objective was to replicate the simplicity of the monks' cells: We wanted to introduce comfort, but not luxury. If you opened the door and saw too much luxury, it would've felt wrong. We also played with the idea of a very practical aesthetic, taken from the Shaker community. The Shakers were interested in linking form and function: They applied their philosophy of sharing and community to objects and thus abided by the concepts of uniformity and standardization. They were a religious community, and this is an abbey, so I played on that.

The design of the iBar, the hotel's bar, is quite similar to a library. Why did you choose to replicate that atmosphere? — We didn't know what to do with that space at first: We thought about making it into a spa, as the idea of water and purification was interesting in this space. Then we wanted to make it a library—somewhere where you could learn something. So we mixed the idea of a bar with the library! It's a place where you can rest, play and still learn, and children can even play a game about the Abbey. That's why this whole project is interesting: It's not ruled by a private company—it's a cultural program.

The dining area has an interesting layout, particularly the side by side seating at some tables. What was the intent behind this? — It's my table for lovers: You are side by side and share the same view. It also means that people don't have to speak too loudly because they are right next to each other, and this increases the feeling of intimacy. Sometimes you remember very simple moments in your life, and this could be one of them.

CHEF — Thibaut Ruggeri

How do you approach creating your menus? — I don't like to work with too many ingredients: Everything on the plate is essential and there for a reason. I like the idea that if you take something away, it would taste completely different. We work with local produce: The meat, wine and vegetables are all from the surrounding regions, and some of the vegetables are even from our own garden in the Abbey. We'll be raising chickens soon as well, so we'll have our own eggs.

How have you arranged the tasting menu? — For me, it's like a concert: You don't ask to hear the last song at the beginning. A menu is exactly the same. I like the idea that you can imagine a progression in your degustation.

What is your favorite dish? — I don't believe in one dish because the meal should be experienced as a whole—you should have a full history on your plate… but the mushroom dish is very popular!

ISSUE TWENTY CREDITS

SPECIAL THANKS
Thanks to Katrin Coetzer for the Starters and Travel illustrations

ON THE COVER
Photographer Pelle Crépin
Photographer's Assistant Mads Emil Sell Langhoff
Retouching Charlotte Player
Styling Carolyne Rapp
Hair and Makeup Line Bille at Agentur using Less is More
Model Cecilie D at Scoop Models
Casting Anja Gildum at Moon Productions
Production The Lab
Digitech Jacob Skaaning
Special thanks to Sofie Brünner, Samuel Åberg at Moon Management and Mai-Britt Jacobsen at Scoop Models

Clothing
Hat by Henrik Vibskov, top by LF Markey and trousers by Studio Nicholson

INTERVIEW: PICO IYER
Special thanks to Kate Runde at Vintage Books

INTERVIEW: ARTHUR GROENEVELD
Clothing
Jeans by American Apparel and vintage sweater

INTERVIEW: DITTE REFFSTRUP
Clothing
Sweater, shirt and trousers by Ganni and sneakers by Nike

INTERVIEW: ABDUL ABASI
Clothing
Shirt, jacket and trousers by Abasi Rosborough

THE NATURALIST: ANITA CALERO
Special thanks to Rebecca McCubbin at Supervision NY, Marco Santucci, Bianca Redgrave and Sophie Walsh at Industry Art, Sarah Lalenya Kazalski and Brooke McClelland at See Management, Sarah Owen and Robin "Che" Torres-Gouzerh

Clothing
Page 50: Her own dress and jewelry
Page 55: Shirt by Studio Nicholson and her own watch
Page 58: Dress by Apiece Apart and her own jewelry
Page 63: Shirt by Studio Nicholson, jeans by Levi's and her own watch
Page 66: Shirt by COMME des GARÇONS
Page 68: Her own dress and jewelry

THROWING SHADE
Photographer's Assistant Mads Emil Sell Langhoff
Retouching Charlotte Player
Hair and Makeup Line Bille at Agentur using Less is More
Model Cecilie D at Scoop Models
Production The Lab
Digitech Jacob Skaaning
Special thanks to Sofie Brünner, Samuel Åberg at Moon Management and Mai-Britt Jacobsen at Scoop Models

Clothing
Page 71: Hat by Henrik Vibskov and top by Totême
Pages 72 and 78: Hat by Co, top by Norse Projects and trousers by COS
Page 73: Hat by Cheap Monday and top by Studio Nicholson
Page 74: Hat by Lock & Co. Hatters and top by Wood Wood
Page 76: Hat by Norse Projects, shirt dress by Hope and dress by COS
Page 77: Hat by Henrik Vibskov and top by LF Markey
Pages 79 and 80: Hat by Weekday, shirt by Filippa K and skirt by Studio Nicholson

BRING IT ON HOME: LEON BRIDGES

Photographer's Assistant Austin Lochheed
Special thanks to Sarah Mary Cunningham at Sony Music, Niles City Sound, Sarah Lalenya Kazalski and Brooke McClelland at See Management and Coco Wolf and Tim Jenkin at Making Pictures

Clothing
Page 88: Suit by Topshop and shirt by COS
Pages 90 and 91: Suit by Sandro, shirt by COS and his own shoes and socks
Pages 93 and 94: His own clothing
Page 96: Jeans by Levi's and his own singlet
Pages 98: Vintage shirt and his own jewelry
Page 99: Vintage shirt, jeans by Levi's and his own jewelry
Page 101: Vintage shirt, trousers by Topshop and his own jewelry
Page 100 (top left): Suit by Topshop, shirt by COS and his own shoes and socks
Page 100 (bottom left): Shirt by COS, trousers by Sandro and his own shoes and socks
Page 102: Jeans by Levi's and his own singlet, shoes and socks
Austin and Josh wear their own clothes throughout

THE ROOM SERVICE MENU

Special thanks to Hotel SP34, which is a part of Brøchner Hotels, and Mario Depicolzuane

Products
Page 104: Lamp by Flos, pens, stapler and tape holder by HAY, clock by Georg Jensen and chair by Carl Hansen & Søn
Page 107: Tray and teapot by Georg Jensen, napkin by Georg Jensen Damask, glass by Illums Bolighus, large plate by Karin Blach Nielsen, small plate by Anette Friis Brahe, cutlery by Gense and cup, jug and round tray by Kähler
Page 108: Lamp by Rubn, notebook by Cinnober, cup by Kähler and stool by Frama

Page 110: Lamp by Rubn, cutlery and carafe by Georg Jensen, glasses by Holmegaard, plate by ferm LIVING and table by Snedkergaarden
Page 112: Bathrobe by Rue Verte, stool by Frama, shaving brush by Acca Kappa, shaving cream, pre-shave oil and body lotion by Barberians and dish by Anne Black
Page 115: Trays by Skultuna, forks by Gense and champagne glass by Rue Verte
Page 116: Tray by Stilleben, plate by Kähler, cutlery by Georg Jensen and napkin by Georg Jensen Damask

A DAY IN THE LIFE: JUSTIN PECK

Special thanks to Katharina Plumb, New York City Ballet and Sarah Lalenya Kazalski and Brooke McClelland at See Management

Clothing
Justin wears his own clothes throughout

ON THE RIGHT TRACK

Photographer's Assistant Istvan Varfy
Hair Adam Szabo at Atomo Management using TIGI
Makeup Sarolta Tombor using Lancôme
Model Sibui at Next Model Management
Digitech Gergely Gönczöl at Flashback Studio
Special thanks to Pierfrancesco Grillo at Atomo Management, Hungarian Railway Museum and Sarah Lalenya Kazalski and Brooke McClelland at See Management

Clothing
Page 130: Coat by Samuji, top by GANT, trousers by COS and bag by USE Bag
Page 132: Shirt by Gucci and trousers by Samuji
Page 133: Dress by Isabel Marant and sunglasses by MANIFESTO
Page 134: Jacket by ÁERON and top by COS
Page 135: Dress by ÁERON

Page 136: Jacket by ÁERON and jumpsuit by Hermès
Page 138: Top by Nanushka, trousers by Samuji and trainers by Converse
Page 139: Top by Paul Smith and trousers by USE Unused

PROFILE SERIES: TAKAHIRO KINOSHITA

Special thanks to Mie Takamatsu and Mako Ayabe

BEHIND THE SCENES: HOTEL FONTEVRAUD

Special thanks to Olivier Châble at Hotel Fontevraud

ISSUE TWENTY PRODUCT STOCKISTS

ABASI ROSBOROUGH
abasirosborough.com

ACCA KAPPA
accakappa.com

ÁERON
aeron.hu

AMERICAN APPAREL
americanapparel.com

ANETTE FRIIS BRAHE
frubrahe.dk

ANNE BLACK
anneblack.com

APIECE APART
apieceapart.com

BARBERIANS
barberianscph.dk

CARL HANSEN & SØN
carlhansen.com

CHEAP MONDAY
cheapmonday.com

CINNOBER
cinnobershop.dk

CO
co-collections.com

COMME DES GARÇONS
comme-des-garcons.com

CONVERSE
converse.com

COS
cosstores.com

FERM LIVING
fermliving.com

FILIPPA K
filippa-k.com

FLOS
flos.com

FRAMA
framacph.com

GANNI
ganni.com

GANT
gant.com

GENSE
gense.se

GEORG JENSEN
georgjensen.com

GEORG JENSEN DAMASK
georgjensen-damask.com

GUCCI
gucci.com

HAY
hay.dk

HENRIK VIBSKOV
henrikvibskov.com

HERMÈS
hermes.com

HOLMEGAARD
holmegaard.com

HOPE
hope-sthlm.com

ILLUMS BOLIGHUS
illumsbolighus.com

ISABEL MARANT
isabelmarant.com/en

KÄHLER
kahlerdesign.com

KARIN BLACH NIELSEN
blachnielsen.com

LANCÔME
lancome.com

LESS IS MORE
lessismore.at

LEVI'S
levi.com

LF MARKEY
lfmarkey.com

LOCK & CO. HATTERS
lockhatters.co.uk

MANIFESTO
manifesto-sunglasses.com

NANUSHKA
nanushka.hu

NIKE
nike.com

NORSE PROJECTS
norseprojects.com

PAUL SMITH
paulsmith.co.uk

RUBN
rubn.se

RUE VERTE
rueverte.dk

SAMUJI
samuji.com

SANDRO
sandro-paris.com

SKULTUNA
skultuna.com

SNEDKERGAARDEN
snedkergaarden.com

STILLEBEN
stilleben.dk

STUDIO NICHOLSON
studionicholson.com

TIGI
tigiprofessional.com

TOPSHOP
topshop.com

TOTÊME
toteme-nyc.com

USE BAG
usebag.hu

USE UNUSED
useunused.com

WEEKDAY
shop.weekday.com

WOOD WOOD
woodwood.dk